Battles Royal

Charles I and the Civil War in Cornwall & the West

H. MILES BROWN

LIBRA BOOKS

First published in 1982
by Libra Books,
27 Fore Street, Lostwithiel,
Cornwall. PL22 0BL
Designed, typeset and printed in Great Britain by
Penwell Ltd, Parkwood, Callington,
Cornwall

©H. Miles Brown 1982
All rights reserved

ISBN 0 9508009 0 2

CONTENTS

Preface

PLATE ACKNOWLEDGEMENTS

1. *King Charles I, 1600-1649. by Lely. Falmouth Parish Church*
2. *Sir Bevil Grenville. by Van Dyck. Jonathan Barker.*
3. *Bradock Church. Jonathan Barker.*
4. *The Redoubt at Boconnoc. Jonathan Barker.*
5. *The Tree Inn, Stratton. Jonathan Barker.*
6. *The Memorial on Stamford Hill. Jonathan Barker.*
7. *Anthony Payne. by Kneller. Royal Institute of C'wall.*
8. *Lanhydrock House. Jonathan Barker.*
9. *The Memorial in Boconnoc Park. Jonathan Barker.*
10. *Boconnoc Church. Jonathan Barker.*
11. *The River Crossing at Cliff. Jonathan Barker.*
12. *Fowey from the Hall Walk. Jonathan Barker.*
13. *Restormel Castle. Jonathan Barker.*
14. *Lostwithiel Bridge. Jonathan Barker.*
15. *Castle Dore. Department of the Environment.*
16. *Lostwithiel Church. Jonathan Barker.*
17. *Lostwithiel Church Font. Jonathan Barker.*
18. *St Nectan's Chapel. Jonathan Barker.*
19. *Pendennis Castle. Photo Precision Ltd.*
20. *Sir Bevil's Memorial, Kilkhampton Church. Jonathan Barker.*

Front Cover: *The Sealed Knot Society in action.*
Adj. Stephen Brown.

Preface

This little book does not lay claim to any original foundation. Its dependence on well-established histories of the Civil Wars and the personalities engaged in them will be plain to see, and acknowledgments to the authors of these works are hereby made; original to this author will be any mistakes or falsity of emphasis.

What this book may claim is the fresh look at the seventeenth-century struggle between King and Parliament in its Cornish situation with the eye of one who has for twenty years lived directly in 'Civil War Country' and whose parishes saw some of the most thrilling and significant actions in the westcountry. The author has walked and pondered on these hills, and by the rivers and bridges, ruminating on the scenes they witnessed, and gaining perhaps some fresh insight into the opposing strategies.

It is my hope that this immediacy may have contributed to the readability, vividness and perhaps even value of the following story of the Civil War in Cornwall.

1982   H. Miles Brown

King Charles I. 1600-1649. Portrait by LELY.

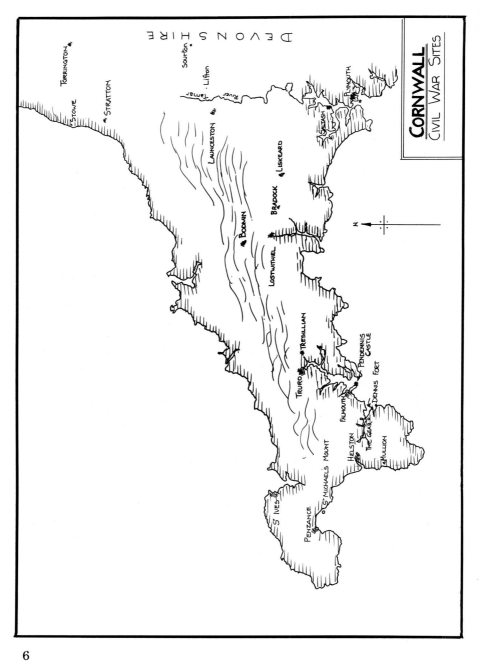

CORNWALL
CIVIL WAR SITES

DEVONSHIRE

Torrington
Bude Stowe
Stratton
Sourton
Lifton
River Tamas
Launceston
Plymouth
Saltash
Braddock
Liskeard
Bodmin
Lostwithiel
Tresillian
Truro
Pendennis Castle
Falmouth
St Dennis Fort
Helston
The Gear
Mullion
St Michaels Mount
St Ives
Penzance

N

CHAPTER 1

The Approach of War

As one walks along the country lanes or views the hills in this peaceful part of the world it is not easy to recall that there was a period when the stone hedges sheltered armed men, there was the sound of battle, the cries of wounded men and the occasional discharge of cannon echoing across the fields. The countryside around seems so far removed from bloodshed and war. Yet some three hundred and forty years ago there were fought in the county of Cornwall some significant battles of the Civil War. Between 1643 and 1648 there were various campaigns mounted, and one of them, the siege of the Parliament troops in Lostwithiel in the high summer of 1644 profoundly influenced the course of the whole war itself.

At first sight it may seem surprising that Cornwall, so remote from London and other great towns, so primitive then in its cultural background, should play an important part in the struggle between King Charles I and his Parliament. In seventeenth century terms, however, the situation was different from that which obtains today. The existence of a number of small boroughs with the right, from time immemorial, of sending two members to Parliament, together with two representing the county itself, meant that a total of 44 members for Cornwall sat in the Commons through Tudor, Stuart and Georgian times, indeed mostly up to 1832 when the Reform Bill of that year swept abuses away.

At any period, and especially in the seventeenth century, there were among these 44 many men of national stature, either Cornishmen who had come to political prominence, like John Eliot of St Germans, a county member from 1628, or outstanding men who had obtained support within the county, like Edward Hyde, a member for Saltash, advisor, and, later as Lord Clarendon, historian of the Royalist cause. Cornwall, in short, knew what was going on.

Another important fact pointing up the significance of Cornwall was the presence of the tin industry, producing a valuable metal vital for the manufacture of cannon and the like, and handy to be traded for other war materials in France, the home country of the Queen, Henrietta Maria. For the first two years of the war she would be there or in Holland tirelessly at work organising the import of tin from western Cornish ports beyond the reach of the navy, which had declared for Parliament.

Parliament, which then represented merely the property-owning and merchant classes, and many of whose Cornish members were elected by handsful of voters in the pay of great families, was subservient to the will of the sovereign. It sat at his direction and call, it was dismissed without its own consent as he saw fit. Its principal function had been to legislate to provide finances for the sovereign's campaigns abroad, or the home defence of the kingdom. Elizabeth and James I had dealt firmly with their Parliaments. In the long reign of the peremptory Queen it had met infrequently and for short sessions. But increasingly there was the flexing of muscles and seizing of opportunities to complain at grievances and attack corruption. Further reform of the Church of England was an increasing concern of the more radical spirits. Elizabeth had kept all this in check, but the pressures were rising.

Charles I came to the throne in 1625, a man strongly imbued with the fatal Stuart ideal of kingly prerogative and the divine authority of the sovereign. This idea was not particularly new; it was however more clearly defined at this time. Charles did not possess the necessary strength of character to sustain this position in the face of the rising power of the elected representatives. As a politician he was devious, indecisive, and secretive, although in personal character he was devoutly a son of the Anglican Church and his family life was above reproach. Kingship was another and separate department of his life, and expediency its watchword in the maintenance of his authority. Weakly and foolishly he continued to allow the influence of favourites in state affairs, particularly George Villiers, Duke of Buckingham, who was in many senses the real ruler until his assassination. Charles, in the rise to power of the extreme protestants was suspected of Popish tendencies. This fear arose both from the presence of a Roman Catholic Queen, and the promotion of William Laud to the Archbishopric of Canterbury, who at the King's desire imposed a much-needed tidying-up on the Church, from cathedrals to village churches. This caused grave misgivings as to its direction.

War with Spain, brought about by Buckingham's intrigues, was accepted at first on an anti-Catholic basis, but the support of the hostilities involved unpopular measures—the levying of taxes, exacting forced loans from each county and so forth. Cornwall was rated for this at £2,000, a considerable sum in the values of those days.

It was reported by the justices that the gentlemen of substance in Cornwall were not able to give in that unconstitutional manner, but would pay 'in a parliamentary way'. When one of the collectors, Sir Francis Godolphin, demanded £10 from Jonathan Rashleigh of Menabilly he told him how unpleasing it was to be employed in that business. Several Cornish gentry were struck off the roll of magistrates or imprisoned for refusing to pay up.

Among the clergy of Cornwall, although most were naturally Royalist in sympathy, there had been unrest for some time, back into Elizabeth's reign. The growth of a radically protestant party, the Puritans, who wanted plain churches, long sermons, a strict Sabbath on Sunday, and a sober way of life imposed by authority, led to a petition from them to Parliament in 1586. It was a small group among the Cornish clergy, but well-informed as to local goings-on, and sure of itself. Bishop Hall of Exeter had dealt gently with this party, allowing an increase of lectureships and kept it in some order; he was delated to the archbishop for this. In 1633 many clergy refused to read in their churches the Declaration of the Book of Sports, which urged the populace to manly games after church on Sundays. This was particularly objectionable to the Puritan conscience, but important for national character.

One of the leading opponents of the royal policies, both inside and outside Parliament, was Sir John Eliot, who was born at Port Eliot, the old monastic house at St Germans, in 1592. Having studied law he commenced his Parliamentary career at the age of 22 with two other prominent radical politicians, John Pym and Peter Wentworth. At the age of 27 Eliot, a county member for Cornwall, was made Vice-Admiral of Devon, and succeeded in trapping the notorious pirate, Nutt. Nutt, however, had influence at court. He was released and Eliot for a while imprisoned. This experience engendered a bitter opposition to the King's mode of rule on the part of Eliot and his friends.

The Parliament of 1628 included among the members many who had suffered as a result of opposing royal policies and actions. Eliot and Pym were eloquent in the airing of grievances, and the Commons responded by proclaiming the Petition of Right, declaring illegal all taxation without consent of Parliament, and imprisonment of any subject of the King without cause shown. Charles was forced to accept this situation. Eliot then began to attack with his fervent oratorical skill the favourite, Buckingham, who in the eyes of many was the chief cause of all the mischief. To the nation's delight, Buckingham was assassinated shortly afterwards. Parliament next turned its attention to Church matters and proposed sweeping reforms. Charles, however, had had enough and determined to end the session and to rule without its unhelpful presence. But the last spurt of Parliamentary opposition lay in resolutions declaring that any who innovated religious matters in a Popish direction, or advised or paid taxes without consent of Parliament, was an enemy of the kingdom.

In retaliation for this Charles imprisoned nine of the leaders of opposition to his policies, ignoring the Petition of Right. Among these nine was Sir John Eliot, who was committed to the Tower. After some time Eliot's health declined, and he died there in 1632. His son requested that his body might be taken back to St Germans for burial. Not least among the grudges held against Charles was his unyielding reply to this plea, "Let Sir John Eliot be buried in the church of that parish where he died".

For eleven years, 1629 to 1640, Charles ruled without Parliamentary help, supported by his chosen advisors, the Earl of Strafford and Archbishop Laud principal among them. It was a period of outward calm, culture flourished and the Anglican Church regained its confidence. It was the period of the Little Gidding venture, with its richness of devotion, the time when many Cornish churches were refurnished and enriched with good woodwork. Underneath all this outward calm and apparent prosperity, however, there was a growing anger. The raising of the funds necessary for government, in the absence of Parliament, was achieved by the imposition of taxes and charges hitherto unknown or long disused.

Among these was the notorious ship-money, raised ostensibly for the defence of the realm against pirates. The western Channel was frequented by predatory ships from Algeria and elsewhere, who in a single month in 1636 captured fifteen fishing boats from Looe and Helford. Ship-money tax was devised by Sir William Noy, a Cornishman of Carnanton, near St Columb. The tax was resented as unconstitutional, although Cornwall found most of the £26,000 demanded in 1634. The navy which should have benefitted from this tax, would prove to be ungrateful as will appear.

Throughout the country, the King made efforts to impose some censorship and control of printed incitements published by various opponents, and to bring the population into acceptance of the royal policies. The court of Star Chamber was empowered, and became for many a symbol of autocracy and terror with its punitive mutilation of such writers as Prynne and others whose works were considered libellous.

In 1637 the King, aided by Archbishop Laud, endeavoured to impose upon Scotland the Anglican—and English—Liturgy for Church worship to replace the Scottish presbyterian mode. There was an immediate and furious reaction to this foolish and ill-con -sidered act. The Scottish nation rose in rebellion and entered into a Solemn League and Covenant for the defence of its traditions.

The period of rule without a Parliament was at an end. In 1640 one was called. It refused to grant supplies, being in general sympathy with the Scots, who then occupied northern England. Charles was forced to sue for a truce. Within a short time this Parliament was dissolved, until later in the year the 'Long' Parliament was convened in the full tide of opposition to the King's policies. It was attended by Cornish members who nourished high hopes of compromise and co-operation with the King, but that was soon seen to be a chimera. Without dissent a series of Acts reducing the monarchy to financial dependence on Parliament was passed. Strafford, the wisest advisor the King had, was attainted and executed. Laud was imprisoned and also went to the block. The system of Church government by bishops was abolished, the attack on episcopacy being led by Francis Rous of Halton, St Dominic, a convinced Puritan. Pym, by a narrow majority, carried in the Commons a long list of grievances against the King—the Grand Remonstrance—dragging up old grudges and some new ones, declaring no confidence in the King. Finally, the last straw was the consideration of a Militia Bill in which the King would be deprived of command of the armed forces, thus placing him in the power of his Commons.

This was too much for Charles. A moderate and Royalist party had begun to emerge in the country and in Parliament in reaction to the extreme policies followed by Pym and his associates. Many felt that the King, although unwisely advised and culpable in many ways, was the focus of stability. Many who once criticised his courts and his taxes began to change their minds in the face of the tactics and opinions of the King's opponents.

Aware of this favourable tide, and perhaps fearful of an attempt to impeach the Queen for her supposed promotion of 'Papist' trends, Charles went to the Commons in January 1642 with a troop of his guard to arrest Pym and four other members. Forewarned, however, these had fled to take refuge in London. There, gathering the train-bands, small units designed for home defence, they returned to Westminster. It was the King's turn to flee. London, where many of the merchants sided with Parliament, was unsafe for him. Compromise was no longer possible. The appeal to force was the sole way forward. Charles issued his Commissions of Array, calling up the militia. He took up his court in York, and in August 1642 raised his standard at Nottingham. The Civil War had begun.

In Cornwall as elsewhere there was dislike of the King's policies, which had led to the running-down of coastal fortifications, in spite of the presence of pirates in the Channel. The impressment of miners and peasants for the Scots war, to the detriment of trade, and the unpopular taxes on the gentry added to the distress. Nevertheless there was a deep reverence for the King's person and the Church of which he was supreme governor. As the issues became clearer men tended to take sides, although for some time the positions were not sharply defined. A man could be a supporter of Parliament yet not be anti-monarchist, and faithfully Anglican. Another might be fervently Royalist and Presbyterian; the few Roman Catholic recusants on the other hand were all of Royalist loyalty, hoping for more freedom under a monarch than was likely under a Puritan Parliament. Parliament itself considered it was, at the outset of the war, not anti-monarchist, but only desired a strict control on the King's activities. As time went on of course the situation changed with the rise of Independency in the Army and the advance of extreme radicalism in Parliament which led to military control of the country in the last days of Cromwell.

At the commencement of the war then, Cornwall in spite of grumbles, took fervently to the King's cause. Most of the great families in the county were Royalists, although some in the eastern parts were supporters of the Parliament.

Leading Royalists included first and foremost the Grenvilles of Stowe, that former remote mansion on the north coast near Morwenstow. Two grandsons of the brave Richard Grenville of the

Sir Bevil Grenville. Had this much loved man survived, the progress of the Civil War may have been very different.

'*Revenge*', who had fought the Spaniards 'at Flores in the Azores' for fifteen hours until his single ship was a wreck and himself forced to yield in 1591, played principal roles in the western wars for the King. Bevil was a man adored—there is no other word—by his contemporaries, his tenants, his servants. At first, as a county member in the Long Parliament of 1640, (and a close friend of Sir John Eliot—he sent to his wife at Stowe portraits of Charles and Eliot) he tended to side with those desiring redress of grievances. But the attack on the King and the approach of war found him wholeheartedly in the Royalist camp. Many who greatly admired Bevil followed. The Governor of the important fortification Pendennis Castle, Sir Nicholas Slanning; John Trevanion of Caerhayes; John Arundell of Trerice; John Trelawny of Trelawne; Jonathan Rashleigh of Menabilly; Sir Richard Vyvyan of Trelowarren; Francis Basset of Tehidy; the Kendalls of Pelyn; the Lowers of St Winnow and Landulph and many others were fervent for the King.

On the side of Parliament from the first were the Rouses of Halton; the Bullers of Morval; William Coryton of St Mellion; Sir Alexander Carew of Antony; Nicholas Boscawen of Truro; and—most importantly—Lord Robartes of Lanhydrock. Some undecided at first or fearing the disturbance of war to their estates and tenants came out eventually on one side or the other. Lord Mohun of Boconnoc and Hall (near Polruan) threw in his lot with the King after some hesitation, and there were naturally others of like late decision.

Lamentably some families were split in their loyalties, some members siding with Parliament while others supported the King. Friendships were sundered and old animosities rekindled. None however forgot they were Cornish, and English. The Civil War did not take on the barbarity and slaughter common in the wars raging at the time on the continent. In fact, the Cornishmen had a name for restraint and mercy in the opening campaigns of the struggle.

Neither at first was there any difference in status between the two opposing factions. Nobility, gentry and simple folk could have been found on either side. It was however not long before the emergence of less cultured and fanatical elements was noticeable on the popular side. While discipline declined among the Royalists, it was strengthened among Parliamentarians as the New Model Army came to the fore in the latter part of the first Civil War.

By way of contrast with Cornwall, Devon, Somerset and Dorset tended more to the Parliament side; although there were fervent Royalist families, these counties were not so homogeneous in their loyalty as was Cornwall. In particular Plymouth early on at the dividing of parties declared for Parliament. It was a strongly Puritan and protestant town. It had something of democratic government in its council. Its seafaring men from the time of the Armada onwards had had experience of the Spanish cruelties and many had suffered under the Inquisition. Their tales, if they returned at all, lost nothing in the telling. At the time when the King was taking counsel of war Sir Jacob Astley was called to his side, being commander of the fortifications and of the St Nicholas Island in the Sound. The mayor and council immediately seized the defences in his absence, and held them for Parliament. During the course of the war the town was beseiged, blockaded, and attacked between 1642 and 1646. The defenders endured much hardship and damage, throwing up outworks and redoubts to protect the walls of the town, which of course was of much smaller size than at present with some 8000 inhabitants. Plymouth was never subdued, and its steadfastness weakened the Royalist cause in the west, since not only were troops necessary for attempts to subdue the town, but also to contain the constant sorties from it into neighbouring Royalist territory.

The story of the Civil War in Cornwall cannot be told without frequent references to goings-on in and around Plymouth, source of many raids and a sure refuge for fleeing Roundheads. Advantageously situated, the town could be supplied from the sea. In spite of Charles's care for the navy, the artful leaders had taken over command and Lord Warwick was High Admiral in the service of the Parliament. The seas therefore were protected for supply to Plymouth. Only further west was there freedom for the Royalist ships, and the employment of privateers for that cause the only hope for their survival. The Sound, that great open harbour, was too wide for the King's guns on either arm of the bay to reach far, and the Island defended the course of ingoing ships to the Plymouth harbour at Sutton Pool. This island, now called Drake's Island, was under the command of Sir Alexander Carew of Antony, and grandson of the author of the *Survey of Cornwall*, which still has power to delight its readers today.

At the outbreak of war the combatants on either side had had no experience of warfare in England and the great majority of Royalists and Parliamentarians caught up into the various armies were initially untrained, with the exception of the small groups enrolled for home defence. Local companies and commands were formed of tenants of the gentry, servants and peasants, either volunteering or pressed into the service of their master, linked to him and the other leaders more by sentiment and ancient loyalty than by appreciation of the niceties of Royalism or democracy.

Through the long period of comparative peace in England there was little available of the necessary apparatus of war. When the struggle began, improvisation was necessary at first. Weapons were hastily fashioned by local smiths, or snatched down from the walls of the manor hall. Armour might consist of a tough leather jacket, a helmet and breastplate, or more complete armour for the wealthier. Anything like uniform issue was lacking until much later in the war and then principally on the part of the New Model Army. Coloured scarves or sashes distinguished Cavaliers from their opponents. Neither was there much uniformity in the armament used. Small-bore guns with romantic names such as sakers, drakes, minions, falconers, demi-culverins fired small shot of up to 9lb and most were much smaller in weight. They had little accuracy and the larger sort were difficult to manoeuvre in a swift-changing field of battle.

Musketeers in both armies were numerous, but again accuracy and rapidity were of low order. Firing was slow, with the need to load the charge, prime, touch with the smouldering match, fire, clean the barrel, and reload. In addition a pronged rest was necessary to support the musket to achieve maximum accuracy of fire. To hit a man at sixty yards showed more luck than skill.

With the accession to the Cavalier side of Prince Rupert, nephew to Charles, and his less brilliant but tough brother Prince Maurice, came a new knowledge of military tactic learned from service in the continental wars in which these and other leaders had been engaged. For instance, previously cavalry charges consisted of waves of single lines of riders moving up to the enemy, discharging their pistols, then giving way to the second line of horse while the first reloaded, and so on. Rupert's experience with the Swedish Army led to his introducing the heavy charge of the whole mass of cavalry armed with pistol, sword or pole-axe to smash through the enemy line. The trouble was that the success of this tactic prompted the joyful cavalry to ride on routing and plundering the fleeing victims, regardless of dire things happening in the rear!

The principal force on either side consisted of the infantry, armed with the pike of some 18 ft length. These weapons could be easily fashioned by local smiths, and the 'push of the pike' was the usual central act of battle after the cavalry charge. In earlier battles of the Civil War the cavalry were marshalled on the wings of the infantry to guard and support them. The Cornish foot troops won high praise for their endurance and compassion, loyally supporting their leaders to whom they were devoted, but growing more and more uneasy the further they marched away from the county border.

Who can blame them? Reliable information was scarce. No letters came. Most were illiterate. They were anxious concerning their homes and harvests, the unfamiliar tones of speech and meeting with less disciplined troops of Royalist armies undermined their confidence, and quarrelsomeness grew. Nevertheless the reputation of the Cornishmen in the Civil War, in spite of some blemishes of vengeful acts after successful battle, remains high and stands in good contrast to the brutality and indiscipline of other troops.

There was of course little or nothing of commissariat. Troops would be quartered or billeted on the local population. Cavalry would be stabled in some local mansion's premises, or for Parliamentarians in some church or cathedral. The countryside would be denuded of provisions to feed soldiers and horses, and although some payment was sometimes promised it was infrequently given.

As early as the late summer of 1642 Sir Richard Vyvyan of Trelowarren, an ardent Royalist, was commissioned to mint coins from gold and silver plate donated or lent for the King's cause, and a Mint was set up in Truro in November 1642. The coin minted there was to be rendered to Sir Ralph Hopton. This Mint, which was probably near the old West Bridge in Truro, had but a short existence, being moved to Exeter on the fall of that city to the Cavaliers in September 1643. Together with the coin minted in Truro from plate supposedly 'loaned' to the King at a rate of interest of 8% there was a weekly assessment of £730 from the Cornish gentry, all intended for the pay of the army. Some of these Truro coins still exist in museums. Soldiers' pay was often much in arrear on both sides of the struggle, and it was a source of complaint just before the battle of Bradock Down that money was owing; some payments made just in time went some way to satisfy the army of the King gathering there.

CHAPTER 2

Bradock Down and Stratton

While it was becoming more and more certain that compromise was not possible and that the King's authority could therefore be maintained only by force there was a good deal of heart-searching among the leading families, and many hoped that if conflict broke out some sort of truce might be found at least in some areas. Local concerns such as the harvest ingathering occupied the minds of many Cornishmen, rather than the distant rumbles of approaching warfare, which it was obvious to all would be so destructive of much they had laboured to produce.

Meanwhile the antagonists commenced manouvering for the allegiance of the towns and the country estates, and to call out militia and trainbands. The King issued Commissions of Array to call up such groups, while Parliament in the light of its Militia Bill, attempted to do the same.

In Cornwall Bodmin and Truro were soon secured for the King, but Launceston was held for Parliament by Sir Richard Buller, of Saltash, who quickly moved up the eastern boundary of the county to seize this county town, where the Assizes were held. Pendennis Castle, commanding the great harbour of Falmouth, was under control of its Royalist Governor, Sir Nicholas Slanning, and St Michael's Mount, equally vital for the western ports, was in the hands of Francis Basset. These important outposts gave shelter to supply ships and privateers for the Royalist cause and enabled valuable war material to be imported into Cornwall. The navy, having declared for Parliament, under Lord Admiral Warwick, could control only lightly these distant points so far from Plymouth.

In Launceston there was an amusing contretemps. In late September 1642 the Assizes were in session. Sir Alexander Carew and Sir Richard Buller brought in a Bill against 'certain persons unknown, who were lately come into the county against the Peace'. These 'certain persons unknown' were actually Sir Ralph Hopton, the King's General of Horse, Sir John Berkeley and Sir Bevil Grenville, who were busy assembling Royalists troops in Cornwall.

These leaders in turn brought in a counter-Bill accusing the Parliamentarian leaders of unlawful assembly. The jury preferred the Royalist Bill, and the small force of Buller's was quickly dispatched across the Tamar. This act marks the opening of serious military operations in Cornwall.

The eastern part of the county was, as it still is, greatly affected by Plymouth and its doings. In this respect it was the decided Parliament loyalty of the town which influenced many leading men in the borderland. Saltash, on the Cornish side of the Tamar, was also an important point. It is more ancient than Plymouth itself —

"Saltash was a borough town
When Plymouth was a furzy down"—

was, and is, the Saltash boast. The little town presided over an important part of the harbour, with ancient rights and privileges over incoming and outgoing river traffic. It was a possible base for attack on the outer defences of Plymouth, or, if held by Parliament, a useful bridgehead for raids into Royalist territory further west or down the Cornish arm of the Sound, where there were Royalist outposts at Millbrook, Maker, and other places early in the war.

At the opening of hostilities Saltash, which changed hands no less than eight times in three years of war, had been seized for Parliament by Scots troops under the command of Col. Ruthven, having been landed from a ship blown into the harbour by high winds. Ruthven was an experienced soldier and respected commander. After the repulse of Carew and Buller at Launceston Hopton followed the river down to Saltash and recaptured the town for the King. Ruthven retreated to Plymouth, where he was given a command.

Sir Ralph Hopton was a straight-forward and warm-hearted officer who had had long experience of warfare in Germany. A moderate Puritan, he was nevertheless unswerving in his loyalty to the King, often in very trying circumstances, as will appear. The force he commanded in Cornwall was small, and if it were to fight outside the county would have to be replaced by volunteer companies. Hopton, Grenville and many others commenced the organising of these, meeting with an eager response. With hastily-fashioned arms and with pay assured by the willing donation of plate for coining into money the Cornish militia began its rise into respect from friend and foe alike. The Parliament opponents dubbed it 'the Cornish Malignants', their favourite name for those loyal to

19

the King, as 'rebels' and 'rascals' were the Royalist taunts for those who took the other side.

Over-confident, Hopton assayed to take his little force across the Tamar and outflank Plymouth by an attack on Plympton, a few miles to the east. Exeter, like Plymouth, had also taken arms against the King, and Hopton was minded to demand its surrender and rally the men of Devon to the Royalist side. Owing to lack of provisions and a successful attack by Ruthven, Hopton abandoned this idea and withdrew to Bodmin. Marching his men back he found Saltash once more against him.

Things thus appearing adverse to their opponents encouraged the Parliament commanders to order two forces drawn from all over the westcountry, one under Ruthven, the other under the Earl of Stamford to march into Cornwall. It was now January 1643. The weather was wintry, the ways muddy for the movement of heavy artillery. Yet it seemed a time ripe for attack, the invasion of Cornwall and the routing of Hopton's weakend force. As in the later campaigns in the far west, it was tempting to assume that if Cornwall could be prised from the Royalist grip the war was as good as won, so important was the county in its strategic position.

Ruthven however was impatient. He decided to cross the Tamar hoping the other reinforcements would catch up with him in time to combine for the attack when he confronted Hopton. It has been suggested that there was also a personal disharmony between Ruthven and Stamford which prompted this foolish decision.

Marching north from Plymouth Ruthven reached Newbridge, the bridge below what is now the village of Gunnislake (but which did not exist at the time). This was then the lowest point at which the Tamar could be crossed on foot. Instead of waiting for Stamford, he pressed on the fifteen miles or so to Liskeard, a town of strong Royalist sympathies. Hopton, although in command of a comparatively small force, decided to attack before the arrival of Stamford and his troops.

By good fortune for Hopton the bad weather had driven three

Bradock Church. ▷

20

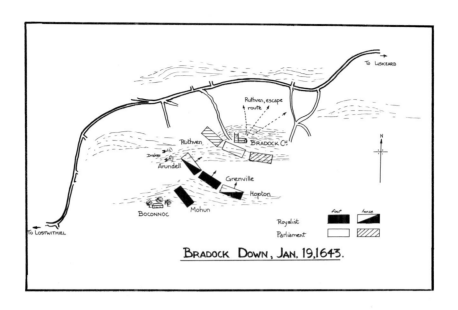

BRADOCK DOWN, JAN. 19,1643.

Bradock Church. Here the Parliament troops assembled for the battle of Bradock Down in 1643.

21

Parliament ships into Falmouth harbour. These ships, quickly over-powered and emptied of their cargoes, provided much-needed supplies for the Royalist companies further east.

Marching deeper into Cornwall, Ruthven took up a position just south of the little church at Bradock, in the high undulating downs about seven miles from Liskeard; these downs then extended from a mile or two from Liskeard almost into Lostwithiel, where the name 'Downend' records how close to the town the wide uncultivated rough area once came. Ruthven guarded his rear by placing musketeers behind the hedges of the road linking the two towns. His chosen position near the church was a strong one. A comparatively level area in front of it falls away sharply to the north, and more gently to the west, with a long sweep to the south, making for easy oversight of the neighbourhood and efficient defence. Beyond the gentler slope to the south the ground rises again to a ridge a half-mile or so from Boconnoc House, then the seat of Lord Mohun, and a Royalist strongpoint.

Coming south from Bodmin, Hopton, Grenville and the other Cavalier leaders bivouacked in Boconnoc Park, probably to the west of the House, with good fires under the hedges. The following morning, January 19, they marched out and about noon came in sight of the Parliament army in strength in front of Bradock church, with the long slope of the hollow ground between them. There was a short interlude of desultory musket shots, neither side willing to relinquish the advantage of their position on high ground. Sir Bevil Grenville was in command of the foot in the centre, facing down the slope, while on his left and right were the horse under Arundell and Hopton respectively. The reserve of foot was placed nearer the House under the command of Lord Mohun. Before the commencement of the battle devout prayers were said at the head of each company.

The Royalists had very cleverly hidden two small brass guns—drakes—which they had taken from Boconnoc House, concealing them in the rough gorse on the left of their position. Ruthven had not had time to bring up and manoeuvre his five large guns into place when the two drakes opened up and surprised the Parliament army.

About two o'clock Grenville led the attack with the foot, following up this surprise with a fierce charge down the slope and up the opposite rise in an unstoppable progress, although their numbers

Boconnoc Redoubt. The obelisk was erected much later but marks the assembly point of the Royalist army for the siege of Lostwithiel.

were smaller than those of their opponents. At the first shock, the 'rebels', already shaken by the sudden discharge of the two little drakes from an unexpected position broke into disorder. The second wave came up after Grenville, the cavalry charged on both wings and turned defeat into rout. The furious men of Liskeard helped in harrying the Parliamentary soldiers, who fled down the steep hill north of the church and along the roads, casting their arms away in desperation. Grenville's men killed two hundred of their opponents, capturing many more. Ruthven's five guns were taken, and the remnant of his force got with great difficulty to Saltash where he entrenched himself until Sunday, January 22. On this day Hopton attacked. The action lasted well into darkness, but at length the town was taken for the King again. Ruthven and his chief officers got away by boat to Plymouth. There was an undignified scramble down the hill to the river Tamar and many were killed or drowned. Eight hundred men were made prisoners, all the stores were taken, as was a supply ship in the harbour which Ruthven had intended as a reserve of arms and stores. Naturally the Royalists were elated at this victory for their strategy, the result of good staff work and throrough follow-up. Cornwall was now clear of 'rebels' for the time.

In the height of his euphoria Grenville wrote to his wife Grace at Stowe:

"My Dear Love,

It hath pleased God to give us a happy victory on this present Thursday, being the 19th January, for which pray join me in giving God thanks—

The next morning, (being this day) we marched forth and about noon came in full view of the enemy's camp, upon a fair heath between Boconnoc and Bradock church. They were in horse much stronger than we but in foot we were superior as I think—I had the van, and so after solemn prayers at the head of every division,I led my part away, who followed me with so great courage, both down one hill and up the other, that it struck terror in them, while the seconds came gallantly after me and the wings of the horse charged on both sides. But their (i.e., the enemy's) courage so failed as they stood not the first charge of the foot, but fled in great disorder, and we chased them divers miles. Many are not slain because of their quick disordering; but we have taken above six hundred prisoners, and more are still brought in by the soldiers—

So I rest,
    Yours ever,
        Bevill Grenville."

One of the King's weaknesses was his disastrous judgment of men, especially of those who should command his forces. Chosen, it would seem, more from consideration of rank than of experience, the incompetence was made worse by his confiding authority to several chiefs at once rather than to one only. Thus in the western command there were at one time no less than four bearing the King's commission as principals. Since many of such leaders were unversed in warfare, touchy and proud, and some dissolute in character, disaster was inbuilt for the King.

One exception was Hopton and his companions in the far west. Hopton was liked, experienced, and a man of integrity. In the Bradock Down campaign and afterwards, Bevil Grenville and Arundell had voluntarily agreed to act as his lieutenants and to accept him as supreme commander. The outcome of the Bradock Down battle was proof of the wisdom of this course of action.

Hopton wished to follow up his victory with the reduction of Plymouth. To this end he mustered strong forces and sent troops to Modbury, east of Plymouth: Tavistock, to the north, and Plymstock to the south-east. The Parliament leaders, however, had not been idle. The men of Devon, Dorset and Somerset, where that cause was far stronger than in Cornwall, were brought together and the Cavaliers were driven from their entrenchments at Modbury, a sortie from Plymouth helping in their defeat. Hopton lost many guns and great numbers of prisoners were taken. Another sortie from the energetic Plymouth defenders drove off Royalist soldiers from the north of the town. The siege of Plymouth was momentarily eased.

In one of the skirmishes to the east of Plymouth in this campaign a stray shot killed Sidney Godolphin, who was slain at Chagford. In the dark the fatal bullet was fired 'from an undiscerned and undiscerning hand'. Godolphin, of the house in west Cornwall of that name, was one of the minor poets of this period. The great historian of the Civil War, the Earl of Clarendon (formerly Edward Hyde, member of Parliament for Saltash) described him as 'a young gentleman of incomparable parts'.

At this point it occurred to a number of the more moderate sort of men on both sides that the moment had come to try to find a way to establish at least a local peace. Parliament did not encourage this sort of piecemeal negotiation, but nevertheless a 'Treaty' was considered by 'Commissioners'. There were meetings at Stonehouse, and at Mount Edgcumbe. The Plymouth Corporation was sufficiently sanguine over this truce proposal as to contribute £10 for their entertainment. It was a natural thing that families, living near one another and intermingled by marriage, business and other interests, who had lived together in amity in a confined area for generations should seize on any chance of avoiding further conflict. Agreement was reached, but representatives were sent down from Parliament to overturn it. There were just two months of cessation from strife.

However, the truce, as is the case in such artifically-patched affairs, was used by the commanders on both sides for the augmentation of their forces. The truce ended on April 22. Hopton had fortified Bodmin with barriers thrown up round the town, while Grenville, Basset and other Cavalier leaders brought companies into Launceston to join Hopton there on the 23rd. The Parliament army was assembled at Lifton, just across the Tamar, commanded, owing to Stamford's illness, by 25-year old Major-General James Chudleigh. Early on 23rd this force attempted to storm the high hill on which Hopton was entrenched. While this activity was in progress, Royalist columns under Mohun, Berkeley, Slanning and Trevanion arrived. Chudleigh was now in a dangerous position, and was on the brink of being cut off at Polson bridge, below the town of Launceston, when a regiment from Plymouth arrived in the nick of time: Chudleigh and his forces retreated to Okehampton almost unharmed.

It was now the turn of the Royalists to taste the bitterness of defeat and rout. Hopton's army now numbered some four thousand men, and it was a propitious moment to march into Devon. In fact, Hopton had no choice, since he had received a letter from King Charles ordering him to march to Somerset to join the Royal army there. This sent Hopton off with enthusiasm, with the chance of chasing the unfortunate Chudleigh and his reduced force from Okehampton. Chudleigh became aware of the approach of the Royalist army at a late moment, too late to do more than try a stratagem. On Sourton Down, not far on the Devon side from the border, he divided his small group of cavalry into units and posted them in hollows in the Downs with orders to charge and make as much noise as possible when the Cavalier Cornish, overconfident, ran into the ambush in the dark.

The suddenness of it all shook the Cornishmen, as from all sides shouting horsemen converged upon them, and with difficulty their commanders managed to regroup them in the shelter of an old earthwork. The enemy by then had disappeared, leaving burning furze to confuse them. While the Royalists were uncertain what to do next, a tremendous thunderstorm broke over them, which proved too much for the superstitious Cornish. In confusion and panic they fled to Bridestowe, where in the morning Hopton collected them to return shamefacedly to Launceston. Left behind were spoils of all kinds, including 1,000 muskets and other material, the most valuable being the despatch case belonging to Hopton, with the King's letter and other correspondence. The King's plan to call Hopton to Somerset was now known to Chudleigh and to Stamford, who had joined in the campaign again.

Stamford, mindful of the order to Hopton to join the King, and realising that things might be serious for the Parliamentary cause if he were allowed to do so, decided to try to prevent the juncture. He collected an army of some six thousand men and led them across the Tamar near Stratton on May 15, sending Chudleigh's father, Sir George, to make a diversion by a raid on Bodmin with a thousand horse. Just north of the village of Stratton lies a spur of high ground running north and south, falling steeply on the eastern side to a little river below, and having a gentler slope to the west where there are still existing some ancient earthworks. Here Stamford took up his position, confident in its impregnability.

Hopton was short of food and equipment after Sourton Down. His men were greatly outnumbered but there was the risk that George Chudleigh would rejoin Stamford and he could hardly afford to wait. Marching north from Launceston he reached Stratton late on the 15th, deciding to attack the next day. Hopton chose as his headquarters the old Manor House, which still exists as the Tree Inn at Stratton and bears a plaque to record the event.

Hopton divided his small army into four groups. Sir John Berkeley had command of the northern group, Sir Bevil Grenville the western, Sir Nicholas Slanning the eastern, while Hopton himself took command of the southern group. The road to Bideford was defended by the horse under Lord Digby.

Early in the morning of May 16 the Royalist assault began. The Cornish foot advanced from the south and west led by Grenville and Hopton, the cavalry covering their rear. Time and time again they charged, firing, reloading, and charging again. Each time they were

27

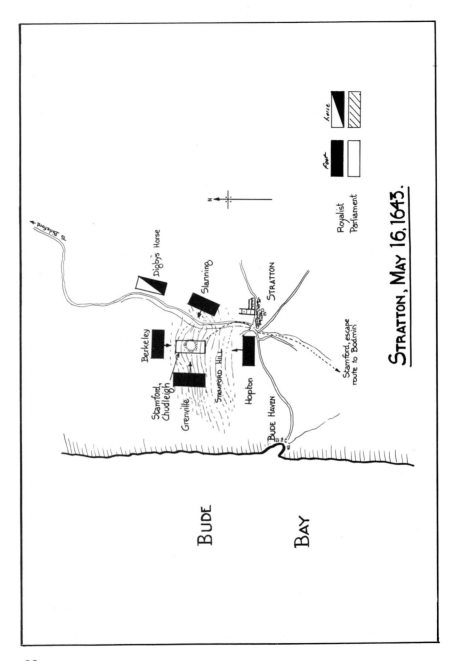

STRATTON, MAY 16, 1643.

Tree Inn, Stratton. H.Q. of Hopton and Grenville. A plaque commemorates the Stamford Hill battle in 1643.

29

thrown back by the Roundheads on the hill, whose cannon, mounted on the earthworks, swept the waves of oncoming Cornishmen. By 3 o'clock in the afternoon the Royalist ammunition was almost spent. Hopton issued the order for a general advance with an attack by pike and sword, holding fire until the summit was reached. The active Cornishmen scrambled up the hill from all directions with devastating effect. Stamford withdrew the horse to Bodmin, while the Parliament men fell back before the irresistable flood of advancing Royalists. Chudleigh was unnerved by the silent swift approach of the Cornish foot, but led a counter-attack against Grenville on the easier western slope. Taking his men too far, he was himself captured. Half-an-hour later the Cornish were over the summit, turning the Roundhead guns on the Parliament men who had retreated into the earthworks, until forced to flee by Grenville, Berkeley and Hopton. Many of the 'rebels' rushed out of the earthworks, down the steep, eastern slope after the retreating cavalry, making for Bodmin. Some, both horse and foot, escaped to Plymouth, that ever-ready shelter for them. This last action had taken scarcely an hour—all was over by 4 o'clock. As a result of this victory, about 1,700 prisoners were captured, with 13 guns and money to a total of £5,000, while the triumphant Royalists suffered only light casualties.

Oddly the hilly site of the battle of Stratton is known as Stamford Hill, which must be one of the few places named after a defeated commander and not the victor! It is a tradition that in the season following the land, ploughed and seeded, yielded a super-abundance of grain by virtue of its having been so generously watered with the blood of the slain.

While Hopton and Grenville were busy at Stratton, Sir George Chudleigh, James's father, and the Parliament horse had attacked Bodmin, which was only lightly defended by the county trained force and some of the townsfolk, who had thrown up barricades. This attack was at first successful. The Royalists were led by 'old Mr Kendall', who was mayor of Lostwithiel that year. Old he may have been, but he put up a good fight, killing ten of Chudleigh's men before he was himself slain. His descendants still live in the Lostwithiel district. But the Roundhead success was short-lived. As soon as the news of the Stratton victory came through the townsfolk rose as a body for the King, and drove the Parliament force in disorderly retreat.

Sir Bevil Grenville was accompanied everywhere by Anthony Payne, his giant 7′ 2″ tall retainer and devoted servant. R.S. Hawker, the famous nineteenth-century vicar of Morwenstow, tells an amusing story of the aftermath of the battle of Stratton. Payne and some others remained after the triumphant leaders had gone, to bury the dead. He caused large trenches to be made, to hold ten bodies side by side. On one occasion they had laid nine corpses, and Payne was bringing in another, tucked under his arm, when the supposedly dead man began to plead piteously, "Surely, you wouldn't bury me, Mr Payne, before I am dead?" "I tell thee, man" was the grim reply, "our trench was dug for ten, and there's nine in already; you must take your place." "But I bean't dead, I say; I haven't done living yet; don't hurry a poor fellow into the earth before his time". "I won't hurry thee. I mean to put thee down quietly and cover thee up, and then thou canst die at thy leisure.".

Payne, of course, was kinder than his speech; he carried the wounded man to his cottage and saw that he was cared for; Hawker says his descendants were among the principal inhabitants of Stratton in his day.

James Chudleigh, having been captured, was deeply impressed by the discipline and morale of the Cornish Royalist troops. A Te Deum was sung in thanksgiving for the victory so unexpectedly given, and the kindness with which he was received moved Chudleigh to change his loyalty and, on promise of pardon by the King, to ally himself with the Royalists. Only a few weeks later Chudleigh's father, Sir George, followed his son's example and changed sides.

Cousin of these Chudleighs was Sir Alexander Carew, who had been placed in charge of the fortifications on the strategically-placed St Nicholas Island, (now called Drake's Island) guarding the inner parts of the Sound and the harbour of Plymouth. Rumours of his cousins' change of allegiance, no doubt distorted, but clear evidence of the goodwill of the Royalists as well as of their success, must have made Alexander deeply consider in his lonely outpost what his own course and future should be. Further anxiety of this sort was to come his way in the next few months. Alexander, the grandson of Richard Carew of the *Survey* does not seem to have held strongly-developed views on the great conflict. His family seems to have been mildly Royalist, but Alexander early took the Parliament side, and was at Launceston with Buller, as will be

The memorial, Stamford Hill, Stratton. Named after the defeated Parliament commander.

Anthony Payne, servant of Sir Bevil Grenville. A big man in every sense of the word, 7'2" tall with matching girth, weighing 38 stone (532 lbs).

remembered. The family portrait at Antony shows a young, thoughtful man, with a rather weak face, hand on sword hilt, and in the buff coat of the Parliament army, breeches and top boots. This portrait reveals a mystery. It has at some time been cut out of its frame at top and bottom, and at some subsequent period carefully stitched back. Obviously the changes of allegiance one way or the other created family discord but it is difficult to say in detail what the circumstances were to bring this mutilation about.

The victory at Stratton opened the way to a brilliant and effective series of campaigns, in which the Cornish militia gained a reputation for their fighting qualities. Hopton marched his three thousand Cornish foot through Devon into Somerset, to join the Royalist cavalry under Prince Maurice. The Somerset towns of Taunton and Bridgwater fell to the newly-reinforced Cavalier army, and at the beginning of July, 1643 the opposing armies met near Bath, which was in Parliament hands under Sir William Waller, a commander of great ability, and poignantly a long-standing friend of Hopton's.

The situation chosen by Waller on Lansdowne hill was not dissimilar to that taken by Stamford at Stratton, and the tactics were also similar. On the Royalist side there were four thousand foot, eight hundred horse and dragoons, and twenty-one guns. Waller's army was smaller, but had been reinforced by Sir Arthur Heselrig's regiment of 'lobsters', so called from the style of their armour. On July 5 Hopton realised that Waller had picked an excellent position, with his infantry behind stone hedges and with his guns trained on the approaching Royalists.

After some preliminary skirmishing and regrouping Hopton sent Sir Bevil and his Cornish foot up the hill to attack Waller's infantry with the support of the horse under Maurice and Lord Carnarvon, followed by musketeers under Hopton. There was much hurt from Waller's guns, and some of the Royalist horsemen fled, but the surviving parties charged five times while the guns of the King's army began to be effective in reducing the Roundhead breastworks. Eventually the Cornish foot gained the top of the hill, the Parliament men withdrawing and pulling away secretly at night, leaving fires and pikes to deceive the Royalists. Although the victory might be that of the Royalists, with great glory to the brave Cornish foot, it was purchased at fearful cost. Sir Bevil, in the moment of victory, was struck down by a blow from a pole-axe; Anthony

Payne, who was at his side, immediately placed his son John Grenville on Bevil's horse, and the Cornish recovered their nerve. Heavy casualties weakened both the opposing forces, but the loss of their beloved leaders such as Grenville fatally undermined the Cornish determination; their loyalty was far more to such local gentry than to the abstractions and philosophies of the Civil War. Further tragedy struck almost at once. Hopton was passing an ammunition cart on which some Parliament prisoners were seated, smoking. The inevitable explosion gravely wounded Hopton, who though not a Cornishman, was regarded with almost equal respect by the militia.

Although a considerable part of Waller's army was intact it was not possible for it to prevent the desperate Royalist advance. Hopton by now was recovering, and after a vigorous defence of Devizes, whose loyal townsfolk reinforced the depleted ammunition stores of Hopton's army, with bedcord match and lead from the church roof, a decisive victory was won at Roundway Down. Waller's army was routed, a thousand were killed and most of the foot made prisoner, although some succeeded in escaping to Gloucester.

The way was now open to Bristol, the most significant town after London, strongly held for Parliament. Its taking would gravely weaken the Roundhead position in the whole of the west. The Royalists from Bath, which had been taken by the victorious Hopton, were now joined by Prince Rupert from Oxford. Bristol was thus surrounded by some fifteen thousand, its garrison only two thousand. Rupert favoured not a siege but a frontal attack, and this was begun on July 26 by the Cornish foot. They faced the strongest defences of the town, ditch and walls too high for the Cornish ladders. After an assault lasting some three hours they were forced to withdraw, having lost in the murderous fire from the walls a third of their number. At this moment Rupert sent word that the walls had been forced on the northern side and called for reinforcements from the Cornish foot. Soon afterwards the town's Governor, Col. Nathanael Fiennes, surrendered and the great city and port was in the hands of the King.

But especially for the Cornish, these campaigns were won at a high price. Only about half of the force remained from the three thousand foot Hopton had led from Stratton a couple of months before; Godolphin, Grenville, Trevanion, Slanning, all killed in the early actions of the Civil War,

'Four wheels of Charles's wain,

Grenville, Godolphin, Trevanion, Slanning, slain.'

Neither was the Cornish army any more the fine fighting unit it had been under these revered leaders, although its reputation was as high as ever; such towns as Dorchester, Weymouth, Portland, Bideford, Barnstaple, and even Exeter were quick to surrender at the very thought of the approach of the feared Cornishmen. It would, surely, soon be the turn of Plymouth.

Sir Alexander Carew, on his lonely post of duty on the Island, watched fearfully the march of events since his cousins had defected from his side. Now with the return of the fabled Cornish and the prospect of an attack on Plymouth, was it not time for him, too, to change allegiance? Carew contacted some Royalist friends. He 'held intelligence by night with Col. Edgcumbe and Major Scawen', probably from the Royalist outpost at Mount Edgcumbe, only a short distance from the Island. He offered to surrender the vital fort of the Island if a full pardon could be obtained from the King. Berkeley, who was besieging Exeter, promised him this and urged Carew to act speedily. Carew insisted on a pardon in writing from the King himself, and in the interval a trusted servant betrayed his design to the mayor of Plymouth. Carew was arrested, and a year later executed on Tower Hill. What might have been the outcome had Carew's plan been carried out is an interesting speculation. Plymouth could hardly have held out and its surrender might so drastically have changed the balance of forces that the Royalist cause might have triumphed, with the whole of the west free from 'rebels' and thus much military might spared for use elsewhere.

Exeter capitulated to Prince Maurice in September, 1643, and except for a few towns apart from Plymouth, such as Poole and Lyme Regis, all the west country was in Royalist hands. From his camp at Sudeley Castle in the Cotswolds Charles sent a 'Declaration to his loving subjects in the County of Cornwall' thanking them for their courage, patience and zeal in his cause, and ordering copies to be sent and displayed in every church in the county. This letter is still to be seen in many of the Cornish churches, often of course replaced later after the Restoration.

It was now to be the turn of Plymouth itself to face the full Royalist strength.

36

CHAPTER 3

Plymouth and Lostwithiel

The Plymouth of the Civil War was of course a much smaller town than the great city of today. It was a walled community, largely still centred on the part round the old harbour of Sutton Pool, extending only to the lower ground below the rise to the Hoe, and barely reaching Drake's Circus, while such parts of the modern city as Union Street, Lipson Vale and Laira, not to mention Devonport, were open marshy areas.

From the commencement of the war the Plymouth people had sensed their importance and their isolation. A number of outer defences were constructed in the country beyond the wall. The principal stockades began at Prince Rock, on the east by the Cattewater shore, to Lipson, Holiwell, Maudlyn, Pennycomequick, the head of Millbay creek and Stonehouse. A continuous earthwork and bank joined all these strong points into an unbroken defence. Today, nothing exists of this, and it is certain the busy traffic up North Hill knows little of the important Maudlyn earthwork once made there, any more than the outbound traffic at Laira realises the sea once crept around to the Lipson valley at high tide, leaving the spur, now Mount Gould, thrust into the water.

As has been mentioned, there had been some vigorous skirmishes in the country around, in which Plymouth played the part of either refuge or place of origin. But it soon became clear more serious trouble was at hand for the Plymouth people. The Parliament disavowal of the local 'Treaty' made it evident there could be no quick end to the war, and so a further strengthening of the walls was ordered.

After the capitulation of Exeter Prince Maurice brought his army further west with the object of reducing Plymouth. Had he not delayed to tackle Dartmouth, there could have been serious problems for Plymouth in view of the depleted state of the garrison. In the interval some five or six hundred men were landed from the sea from Portsmouth, reinforcing the locals. Among these incomers were two brilliant commanders, Colonels Wardlaw and Gould. On these two would rest much of the responsibility for the defence of the town so vigorously maintained throughout.

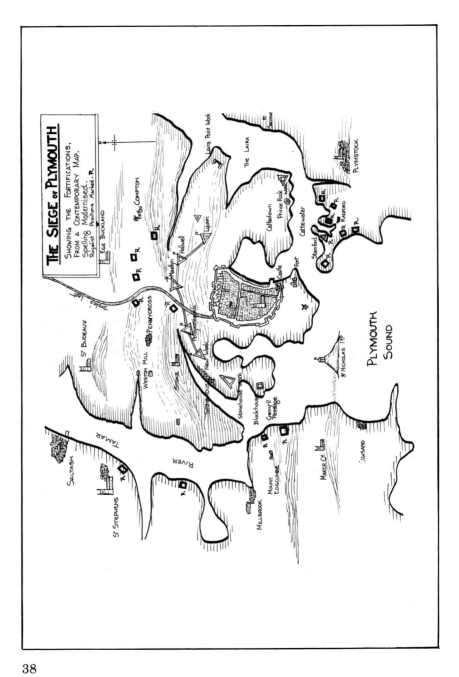

Maurice arrived at a time when Wardlaw had already made one or two minor but successful raids on neighbouring Royalist points, believing that the best part of defence is attack. But Maurice's army was formidable in its strength. The Prince made his headquarters at Widey Court (now demolished by uncaring townsfolk) and deployed no less than five regiments of horse and nine of infantry in a great half-circle from the Cornish coast at Cawsand to the Devon coast at Plymstock. To the watchers on the Plymouth walls the sight must have been sobering indeed. The first attack was on a bravely-held Parliament point at Mount Stamford, within sight of the Hoe, but when over-run this spot was found to be useless for attacking strategy.

Prince Maurice issued an impressive 'Proclamation' to the people of Plymouth, signed by a long list of prominent Cornish leaders—Bassets, Killigrews, Prideaux, Trelawnys, Arundells—promising security from plunder and a general pardon if the town surrendered to the King. This Proclamation had anything but the desired effect. It stiffened to a remarkable degree the determination of the townsfolk to defend their homes, and many who were of doubtful loyalty to the Parliament cause were arrested. In true Puritan fashion a 'Solemn Vow and Covenant' was proposed to be taken by all on a special 'Day of Humiliation', binding the populace together and uniting them as never before. They swore to defend the forts and the Island, to give up no part of them without the consent of both Houses of Parliament, and to accept no protection from the 'enemy'. No oath could have been more solemn to an intensely Puritan community. After this was done, work began with a will to strengthen the stockades and earthworks still more.

The Plymouth people did not have to wait long for the greatest threat from the Royalists to materialise. The chosen day was Sunday, December 3, 1643. Maurice planned to set in motion a large army on the eastern perimeter of the town and to march from the Lipson valley to storm the Lipson Work further up the hill between the valley and Plymouth beyond the slope. Once over the summit the town would be at the mercy of the Cavaliers. During the Saturday night two 'traitors', the Parliament term for them, guided Royalist detachments through the marshes of the east end of the valley, reaching the low ground below what is now Mount Gould.

There was a little Parliament outpost there at Laira. This was now overrun, but not before it was able to sound an alarm. This alerted the garrison at the Lipson Work on the hill, and its commander was able to reinforce his numbers to 150 horse and 300 foot, a feeble opposition to the greater Cavalier strength, which stood at a majority of ten to one. These reinforcements gathered just below the summit of the ridge on the Plymouth side, and could not be seen by Maurice at Compton.

They could however be seen at daylight from Mount Stamford, and the Royalists there fired a warning gun. The Cavalier army began to move. It poured in a mass from Compton north of the valley down into Lipson Vale with the objective of getting within pistol-shot of the Lipson Work near the top of the ridge. For some time the Royalists waited under the hedges. On summoning the Work to surrender, all they got in reply was a defiant cannon-shot. The Cavalier army then advanced up the hill to the top. Some last few reinforcements, only another 200 men, were sent up from the town, while a drake began to rake the Cavalier lines. A party of 60 musketeers was sent quietly round behind the end of the ridge of Mount Gould to surprise the Royalist rear. At the signal of a drum-beat Wardlaw ordered a general assault. At the same time as the pitifully thin line of Roundhead soldiers ran forward from the summit of the ridge the musketeers opened up. Caught between these two fires the Cavalier army broke and panicked. Their retreat carried Maurice's men down the precipitous slope into the Laira creek. By then it was high tide and flooding with water. Horses and men were struggling in the muddy flow and scores were drowned. The flight became a rout, men fleeing anywhere, and anyhow. Hundreds were captured.

The transformation was complete. Far from receiving the abject surrender of the town, the Royalist threat was shattered in this disaster of the 'Sabbath Day Fight' of December 3, 1643. Plymouth still remembers this date and this deliverance, naming the ridge on which it was won 'Freedom Fields', with a monument in Freedom Park to the bravery of the townsfolk. 'Prince Maurice Road' in the same neighbourhood marks the path of Royalist flight today.

Cavalier successes after this were small, although they did succeed for a time in taking great toll of the defenders of the Maudlyn Work at the top of what is now North Hill, but were driven off with many casualties. Maurice's hope of subduing the town by Christmas Day was dashed. Finding that his army was weakened by loss, sickness and suffering through the bad weather, he marched away, ending his active campaign around Plymouth.

The serious attempt at a siege of the town being thwarted did not mean the end of anxiety for the inhabitants, since a land blockade was instituted instead. This was first set up by Col. Digby, who shortly after the beginning of 1644 gave place to Sir Richard Grenville, brother of Sir Bevil, but a man of entirely different stamp. Nothing except his military skill, learned in the continental wars, recommends Sir Richard, whose reputation for brutality and touchiness outlives his undoubted loyalty to King Charles. But, that said, men were proud to serve under him.

At the outset of the war Richard Grenville had declared for Parliament, and spent some months in London consulting with the Commissioners about the defence of Plymouth, with the prospect of becoming its Governor. He was given the sum of £600 and a troop of horse. Setting out for the westcountry, with a coach and six horses, a wagon with more horses, and servants, Grenville arrived at Bagshot. Here in an eloquent speech he described his abhorrence of rebellion and warring against the anointed sovereign, inviting his troops to follow him into the King's service. With the majority of his followers Grenville rode to Oxford, joining the King and handing to him all the plans which the Parliament command had entrusted to him. The chagrin and fury of the Parliament leaders at this betrayal can be imagined. Grenville's reasons for switching sides were his disillusionment with the development of the political activities on the popular side, and the assertion of privileges far beyond those claimed by earlier Parliaments. These developments were to accelerate and unsettle many others in the same way.

The reaction of Parliament was violent. It had two gibbets erected, with a proclamation nailed to each describing Richard Grenville as 'traitor, rogue, villain, and Skellum', and declaring the gibbets were placed in intention and hope that Grenville would grace one of them, either that in Palace Yard, Westminster, or the other at Royal Exchange. 'Skellum' is the title that has stuck as a nickname of this man even to this day.

Sir Richard Grenville arrived in the west in March 1644, and due to an accident which prevented Col. Digby from continuing the blockade of Plymouth Grenville was empowered to command in his place. The town had grievously suffered in the period of the siege and assaults, and was short of water, the Royalists having cut Drake's Leat which supplied the needs of the population. Supplies of food were scanty, too, but a 'miraculous' inflow of shoals of 'pilchards', or more probably mullet, enabled the inhabitants to scoop them up in baskets. (The author remembers a similar occurrence in about 1920, when he too took home an ample supper easily obtained in this way.)

The blockade brought a little easier time for the town than in the siege, but there were constant forays keeping the garrison busy, and constant danger from Royalist guns placed at Mount Stamford. Both Gould and Wardlaw having died the Plymouth command was now held by Lieut-Col. Martin, an energetic and resourceful officer. His policy was to attack wherever the blockaders made a concentration of troops, and following this policy he stormed the fortified tower of St Budeaux church, captured three guns from a blockhouse at Mount Edgcumbe, and attacked Maker Church, where the Cavaliers had fortified this useful look-out. A fort at Cawsand, and entrenchments at Millbrook were attacked and an attempt on Saltash also featured in the strategy of Martin. Two hundred prisoners, much spoil, and general heartening of the garrison were the results of these forays, which however much they kept the blockaders on the alert were only on a small scale. John Syms, a Puritan minister whose diary of this period is invaluable as a historical source, mentions that the purposes of these excursions were principally to replenish the food and fuel supplies, and that several took place every week.

It is clear however that the blockade maintained by Grenville was having some effect. Martin was compelled to send appeals to London for money, clothing, and powder for the artillery, and although ships could get into the harbour it was at considerable risk from the Royalist cannon planted at such spots as Mount Stamford overlooking the principal landing places. But the effect of the Cavalier blockade came just short of starvation, and the town's inhabitants had just enough to survive. It was to some extent a stalemate.

In June, 1644 however this was suddenly broken with the news that the General of the Parliament army, Robert Devereux, Earl of Essex, (who incidentally was a former comrade-in-arms of Richard Grenville in Germany) had begun to move into the westcountry with a Roundhead army of some eight thousand men. Before Essex's advance Prince Maurice, who was besieging Lyme Regis, had to retreat to Exeter. Essex coming on his heels hoped to capture the

Queen, who was in residence there; she however fled the country and retired to France. Taunton and Barnstaple quickly surrendered to Essex. It was not a propitious time for the Royalists. Elsewhere too the Royalist cause seemed to be crumbling fast, and the war moving into a more bitter stage with quarrels among the King's commanders, and the emergence of fanatically-nourished factions on the other side. The more moderate men were either dead or out-shone by extremists. Those with important commands or great political influence took charge even in opposition to Queen, Rupert, or, on the other side, Parliament itself. The war was generating its own momentum. In addition the Scots were now brought into the struggle, and the eastern counties' armies were being forged into mightily effective forces from which the New Model Army more homogeneously ordered and commanded was to emerge. In early July 1644 came the shattering news of the defeat of the Royalist army at Marston Moor a few miles west of York, and the surrender of that city to Parliament. The tide of the war was unmistakably turning against the King. But it was not yet over, nor was there still victory for him lacking in loyal Cornwall.

In response to an appeal from Plymouth, Essex marched his men to its relief in mid-July. This move made it necesary for Sir Richard Grenville, with his smaller forces to retreat into Cornwall, which he did via Horsebridge on the Tamar, hoping but in vain that he might also block Essex's possible advance into the county. Some two thousand men had reinforced Essex's army, and it was now that he accepted the advice of Lord Robartes of Lanhydrock to come into Cornwall to try to persuade the Cornish to surrender to him. Robartes told him that the people were tired of the war, and only desired peace so as to get the harvest in. They would, said Robartes, welcome his army if Essex showed himself reasonable. This was, as it turned out, an invitation to disaster on the grand scale, but Essex naturally supposed Robartes to know the mood of the people in Cornwall.

This John Robartes was the second to have held the title. His father Richard had been a member of an enterprising merchant and banking family in Truro, largely profiting by the tin trade. Buckingham, James's and Charles's favourite, as a means of raising money was at the time compelling prosperous persons to purchase titles or pay a fine for refusing. Robartes—this spelling was adopted from the original Roberts—paid £10,000 for the barony. In 1620 he

Lanhydrock House. The seat of Lord Robartes who misjudged the mood of the Cornish and unwittingly led the Earl of Essex into a trap.

purchased the manor and advowson of Lanhydrock and commenced the building of the House there, although he never lived in it. His son John completed the work just before the outbreak of war. John was, in the Lords, a respected leader for the Parliament cause. It was not surprising that Essex trusted his advice. On July 20 1644 Essex crossed into Cornwall at Horsebridge, forcing Grenville further west.

There was indeed to some extent a disillusionment with the war and its effects, as Grenville found when, first at Truro and after at Penryn, he tried to increase the Royalist strength by calling up serviceable men. The ready response of the first year of the war was lacking. Then, dramatically, the whole picture changed. The King wrote to Grenville announcing his arrival in the westcountry, his approach unopposed since he had successfully overcome resistance by Waller at Cropredy Bridge.

With Prince Maurice's men, whom he planned to join on Caradon Hill, the King could command some fifteen thousand men. Essex would find himself the hunted, not the hunter. In the west, now moving towards him was Richard Grenville and his army. Behind him, inexorably approaching, was the King with his powerful troops. Instead of chasing a demoralised enemy Essex was between the two jaws of a vicious pincers. And the actual presence of the King, who was accompanied by his son, the fourteen-year old Prince of Wales, transformed the mood of the loyal Cornish into one of enthusiastic support.

Essex then with 10,000 troops entering Cornwall after a short skirmish took Launceston and Saltash, and made for Bodmin. Only eleven days afterwards the King was at Launceston with 2000 foot, 5000 horse, and 28 cannon. On Thursday, August 1 His Majesty stayed at Trecarrel, the house of Ambrose Manaton, a strong Royalist.

Considerable interest, and not a little vividness, attaches to the subsequent action in mid-Cornwall from the survival of a day-to-day diary of the skirmishes and incidents made by a Royalist officer, Richard Symonds. Subsequently published this diary enables us to follow the development of the strategy of the Lostwithiel campaign from the Royalist side. It is a pity that no corresponding source is available from the other in so direct a fashion.

By August 2 Essex had penetrated the long peninsula between Bodmin and Fowey taking the latter town and harbour, and setting up his headquarters at Lostwithiel, an ancient borough town of about 800 inhabitants. In the meantime the King had marched his men to Liskeard, making his own base at the house of Joseph Jane,

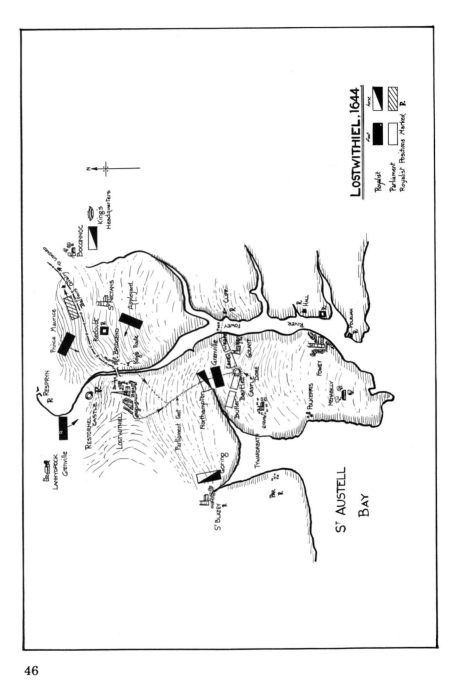

LOSTWITHIEL. 1644

Royalist
Parliament
Royalist Positions Marked R.

foot | horse

King's Headquarters

BOCONNOC

To LANGORE

Prince Maurice

R. RESPRYN

Grenville

LANHYDROCK

RESTORMEL CASTLE R.

ST NECTANS

REDOUBT R.

ST. BRIDGEND

King's Rode

Appleyard

R. CLIFF

Fowey R.

R. HALL

R. RIVER

R. DULOAN

LOSTWITHIEL

Parliament Foot

Northampton

Grenville

Butler

Castle Dore

GOLANT

FOWEY

Restormel

MEVAGILLY

POLKERRIS

TYWARDREATH

Goring

ST BLAZEY R.

PAR R.

ST AUSTELL BAY

46

a strong Royalist who was MP for Liskeard, an intensely loyal town, as we have seen. Jane's house is still in existence in Liskeard. Named now 'Stuart House', this slate-hung building in the main street bears a tablet recording that Charles lodged there from August 2—7 and on September 4, 1644.

An amusing incident occurred on the following Sunday, August 4. Some countryfolk had complained to the King that Essex's men were plundering the countryside for provisions and fodder. The King sent out a party of soldiers to drive them off. To them came a small Cornish boy who told them of 'many gay men' at Lord Mohun's house. It was soon apparent that in his absence Lord Mohun's house had been taken over by men of the Parliament, and that a good carousing time was being had there. Although they had eighty musketeers supposedly on watch, the house was surprised, and many captured in their drink or sleep, including a Col. Aldridge. The Quarter-Master General to Essex, Dalbier, a Dutchman, was quick in his reaction to the noise at the door, being neither asleep nor drunk. He threw off his hat and scarf, seized a servant's apron and a couple of pots, and so escaped scrutiny and made off without challenge, being supposedly a serving-man.

By Thursday August 8 the whole of the King's army was on Bradock Down in full strength. It must have made a brave sight, with the colours of the companies, the bright caparisons and flowing plumed hats, shining armour, and stands of pikes, with the dashing of cavalry here and there. And among it all, the King himself, in personal command of the only campaign in Cornwall in which he himself was present. The country folk must have seen a sight not easily to be forgotten. On this day Lord Goring was made General of Horse in the place of Lord Willmott. This was hardly a good omen for success, as Goring was a notorious drunkard, and Grenville was later to accuse him of sluggish response to vital commands. However on that day the Parliament horse was beaten back from its display on the hills near Lostwithiel, while the next day the rebels' cannon started to fire at the Royalists from two pieces they had brought up.

Prince Maurice now moved up to Boconnoc and Lanhydrock, sending a letter to Essex suggesting that he should leave the Parliament side and come over to His Majesty, and proposing a treaty of peace. This letter had the extra point that it was borne by Lord Beauchamp, a nephew of Essex. About 10 the next day, August 10, the reply came back:—

"My Lords,
    In the beginning of your letter you express by what authority you send it; I having no authority to treat without

the Parliament who have entrusted me, cannot do it without breach of trust.

Your humble servant,
    Essex.
From Lostwithiel Aug. 10 1644."

About this time there took place an incident which is recorded by Hals, the Cornish historian, from the personal evidence of some who had taken part in it. While the two armies were in close contact on Moylesbarrow Down, in St Winnow parish, a 'Skirmish by Challenge' took place. Colonel Straughan, of the Roundhead army issued the challenge which was accepted for the Royalists by Lord Digby for the King.

Straughan's troop consisted of one hundred young men, from sixteen to twenty years of age, all double-if not treble-armed for the encounter. Straughan himself led the attack, clad only in a hat and a shirt (briefly the weather may have been hot). Here, after an interval in which they showed off, Lord Digby and his troop came forward with resolution and bravery, but fired their pistols off too soon, and did little damage to their opponents, who then advanced and fired so close to the Royalist youths that half of them were killed on the spot and nearly all received some injury. This account was given to Hals by William Maye, who was in Digby's troop (and died in 1672) and two brothers, Joseph and William Upcott, who were with Straughan.

The King set up his court and headquarters at Boconnoc, attending service in the church there on Sunday August 11. The same day there was consultation between the commanders, Hopton meeting with Grenville, who came to the King, leaving his army raising fortifications around Bodmin.

The presence in the neighbourhood of strong Royalist forces gradually moving in towards them caused the Parliament group holding the bridge at Respryn to withdraw, thus leaving open access for their opponents to have free passage between the two parts of the Cavalier army. The bridge at Respryn was undamaged, and its significance can easily be realised by the many visitors to this beauty spot today.

Essex appears to have been culpably slack in not gaining control of the salient points around his contracting position. All down the east side of the river Fowey one by one the passes and strong points passed into Royalist hands, and supplies for his troops from Fowey

Boconnoc memorial. Site of the "Struggle of Challenge"?

were gradually cut off. The Puritan minister John Syms tells us in his diary that he was appointed chaplain on the *Providence*, a man-of-war sent from Plymouth with supplies, setting sail on 4 August and landing provisions at Fowey. But one ship could not possibly meet the needs of Essex's large force, and the deteriorating weather with west winds, presaging rain, prevented further ships getting into Fowey harbour even when it was open. Syms also records how his ship engaged a Royalist ship near Falmouth, and during the exchange of fire a cannon ball entered a porthole narrowly missing Syms, glancing off a brass gun and injuring a wounded man to whom he was ministering.

Perhaps not all the supplies landed for Essex's army got to their destination as Richard Symonds mentions that Sir Jacob Astley captured two butts of sack, tobacco, and horse shoes coming to the 'rebels' from Fowey. It was Astley who at the battle of Edgehill uttered the well-known prayer—

"Lord, thou knowest I shall be very busy this day. I may forget thee. I pray thee, do not thou forget me."

A shrewd man, he survived to mock the Roundhead soldiers who had captured him after a skirmish at Stow-on-the-Wold, prophesying the victors would fall out among themselves.

Further west, Grenville made approaches towards Essex's position, which was steadily worsening. Lanhydrock House was seized by the Royalists, and it is a reflection on the customs of war at that time that Prince Maurice, according to Symonds, hanged a man for plundering there since a protection had been given by the Cavaliers to Robartes's property. However, Grenville seems to have taken much from the house and the many bows and arrows found there were no doubt commandeered. All Robartes's silver was packed off to the Royalist Mint.

In the manoeuvring around the town the Royalists nearly succeeded in blowing up the Parliamentary ammunition wagons, the burning fuse being discovered when only two inches away from the powder. Essex's complaint to Parliament displays his feeling that this sort of warfare was hardly gentlemanly!

Bad weather arrived on August 15, blustering and wet, and this lasted on and off for the whole campaign. By the 17th the parlous situation in which Essex found himself was becoming obvious. According to two of his soldiers who were captured, provisions were already scarce in the Roundhead army.

Boconnoc Church where Charles I attended service during his stay in the area on August 11th 1644.

Three or four miles down river from Lostwithiel there was a pass over the water from Golant to Cliff, in St Veep parish. This pass at Cliff was held for the Royalists by Col. Lloyd's regiment. To strengthen this hold on Saturday, August 17 His Majesty accompanied by troops of the Queen's force commanded by Capt. Brett, marched down the steep road to Cliff overlooking the Golant side of the peninsula in which Essex was slowly being confined. Further down the river Hall, a seat of Lord Mohun, was secured by Astley with a detachment of 200 to maintain it. The neighbouring Hall Walk, nowadays an attraction for visitors, was used to mount several of the largest Royalist guns, as was the fort at Polruan at the mouth of the harbour, effectively sealing it to prevent supply ships coming in.

The King came to inspect these fortifications on August 17. While he was there a shot from a musket in the town killed a fisherman where the King had just passed by.

Further north around Lostwithiel during misty weather the King's and Prince Maurice's armies got on the high hills over-looking Lostwithiel on the eastern side, the two commanding emin-ences of Beacon Hill and the hill opposite Restormel Castle. Later on August 21 the Royalists got a party on top of the hill next to Lostwithiel, at the foot of which was the hamlet of Bridgend, now a suburb of the town. Grenville surprised the Roundhead garrison at Restormel Castle, the ruins of which were still an important outpost commanding Lostwithiel, finding there thirty 'rebels' and 'divers barrels of Beefe'. The Roundhead garrison, under Col. Weare, gave up without much opposition at the approach of the Cornish militia under Grenville.

The small cottages at the foot of the hill in Bridgend were on fire, the thatched roofs making the spread of the fires a foregone conclusion in the windy weather and there was vigorous cannon fire from the Roundhead side, but resulting in 'no great hurt' to the besiegers.

Essex and his army were now in an impossible position. They were bottled up in a narrow peninsula about five miles long, between Lostwithiel and Fowey, and a couple of miles wide. The sea came inland much more than at the present time, up to Treesmill and near St Blazey. The upland was largely heath. There were only small holdings, with the exception of the great estate of the Rashleighs, Menabilly, and the town of Fowey itself. There was not enough

Cliff. A gunsite overlooking the River Fowey. Roundhead cannonballs have been used to decorate the front of the cottage.

53

Hall. A favourite walk today. From here it is possible to visualise what an easy target the town of Fowey and the harbour would have been for the Royalist cannons.

Restormel Castle. Not "one of the ruins that Cromwell knocked about a bit". It was already like it, but still a commanding stronghold overlooking Lostwithiel.

55

provision for the multitude of men and horses needing food, shelter and warmth. In the period of the siege the whole of the available goods of houses, estate and stores was commandeered for the supply of the Roundhead army. Menabilly was stripped and plundered, the townsfolk of Fowey and Lostwithiel had soldiers billeted on them, there were constant forays to seize cattle and livestock of all kinds. There was no hope of escape or supply from the sea, as the Royalist guns commanded the port, and the weather prevented any attack by the Parliament navy. To cross the river Fowey was rendered impossible by the strategic placing of Royalist troops at every point at which such a venture might be made.

Towards nightfall on the 21st the Cavalier troops of the King's army got into the fields on the eastern outskirts of Lostwithiel. Near St Nectan's chapel a party under Col. Appleyard, consisting of 1000 foot, reinforced the armies on the other hills under Prince Maurice and Lord Brentford. On the Thursday night in the misty dark an earthwork twenty yards square—the King's Redoubt—overlooking Lostwithiel was dug and cannon planted there to fire into the town. When daylight came it revealed this new work, the freshly-turned earth appearing as if it were a close-packed body of horse on the very verge of their position, and the Roundhead cannon shot off many 9 lb roundshot at this earthwork, with but little effect. This bombardment continued the next day, St Bartholomew's day, the day of the patron saint of Lostwithiel church. In the corresponding reply from the Royalist pieces the tower and spire of the church were damaged, but news came through to the King that the 'rebels' had begun to make for Fowey in force.

It turned out that this was a regrouping preparing for an attack from the Cavalier western army, under Basset and Goring, who had seized the little port of Par, St Blazey, and St Austell. No relief was possible from that quarter for Essex, since some 2000 horse and 1000 foot of the King's army had got round to the west of his position. In the event Essex abandoned any plan to attack in this quarter.

In his camp at Boconnoc the King had news late on Friday, August 30 that the Roundhead army had begun to withdraw from Lostwithiel and the surrounding area. His all-too-shortlived triumph was about to begin.

CHAPTER 4

Escape and Defeat

The Earl of Essex had hoped for relief to come from Lieut-General Middleton's force in Somersetshire. This hope was destroyed by Sir Francis Doddington's success over Middleton at Sherborne. The Parliamentarian outlook was now bleak indeed. Essex convened a Council of War in Lostwithiel, possibly in what is now Edgcumbe House in the main street. It was determined that Sir William Balfour should endeavour to lead the cavalry through the King's forces, and that Essex should try to embark the foot at Fowey and escape with them by sea, hopefully to Plymouth with assistance from that town.

The night of Friday, August 30 was foggy and wet, with that peculiar opaqueness dwellers in Cornwall know well. To protect the road from Lostwithiel to Liskeard the Royalists had posted fifty musketeers in a cottage hard by the way with instructions to keep watch. The night was dark, the risk supposed to be slight, the cottage was warm and the refreshments enticing.

On either side of the cottage up in the hills and separated by scarcely a musket-shot were the two armies of the Royalists, warned and standing to their arms all night. About 3 o'clock in the morning the whole of Essex's cavalry, to the number of 2,500, no doubt with hooves well-muffled, slipped through the Cavalier lines without a shot being fired or any alarm given. With the cavalry was a number of Cornish Parliament notables, Col. Nicholas Boscawen, Lieut-Col. James Hals, of Merther, Henry Courtenay of St Benet's in Lanivet, Col. John St Aubyn of Clowance, Lieut-Col. Braddon, Col. Carter and several other 'gentlemen of quality'.

When day broke, this cavalcade was spotted well to the east of Lostwithiel passing over the downs north of Liskeard. Pursuit was hampered by the fact that several parties of Royalist command were out foraging for food. Clevedon's brigade was the only one available, and came up with them, attacking the rear of the Roundhead cavalry and killing several men. Others, whose horses were tired were taken prisoner. The main body of Roundheads, frequently making a stand, beat off their opponents and safely got

Lostwithiel bridge. A mine planted under it was dismantled in time to prevent retreating Roundheads from blowing it up.

to Plymouth. There were bitter Royalist recriminations at the success of this bold venture of Balfour's.

It was now necessary for Essex to extricate the foot. He drew them together and began the march up the steeply hilly ground west of Lostwithiel, having previously mined the ancient bridge over the river in the town to prevent the Royalists overtaking them as they went.

At about 7 o'clock in the morning of the Saturday the King's men entered Lostwithiel, the mine, whose installation had been observed, having been rendered harmless to allow their progress over the bridge. No doubt the inhabitants were there in force to greet their deliverers in hope that their privations were at an end. The King was approached by a local man, one Stephens, an officer in his army, who knew of a crossing-place over the river Fowey south of the town. Using this short cut they would outflank the retreating Parliament troops. Before leading the way the King, out of gratitude for this suggestion, took from his satchel a silver cup and presented this to Stephens as a reward for his assistance. The cup is still in existence in the keeping of a Cornish family. It is a plain goblet about six inches tall and three in diameter at the top.

This outflanking move resulted in the capture of a cartload of muskets and five cannon, two being very long ones, left in the mud. Essex, explaining later the progress of affairs said—

'the ways were so extreme foul with excessive rain and the harness of the draught horses so rotten that in the marching off we lost three demi-culverins and a brass piece and yet the Major-General (Skippon) fought in the rear all day he being loth to lose those pieces, thirty horses were put to each of them, but could not move them, the night was so foul and the soldiers so tired that they were hardly to be kept to their colours.'

The two pursuing groups of Royalists, those who crossed the river and those who marched through the town, joined up and continued the advance together, the Parliamentarians resisting strongly and making a stand now and then. Their musketeers set up their rests in the soggy ground firing off volley after volley to deter their pursuers. There was a spirited Roundhead attempt to get across from Golant at the St Veep pass at Cliff, but this was beaten off. Some cannon balls from this Roundhead effort remain at a cottage at Cliff. Along the high ridge of the peninsula the main body of the

Castle Dore from the air. Ancient site reputed to have been the castle of King Mark. Here the surrender of the Parliament army was received by King Charles on 1st September 1644.

dispirited Parliament foot straggled in some sort of order until the old hill fort of Castle Dore was reached.

This ancient earthwork consists of an immense circular area surrounded by a bank and ditch, eminently suitable as a strong point, and from its high position the surrounding countryside was easily surveyed. Essex decided that a stand should be made here. He first considered that the ammunition wagons should be sent on to Menabilly if possible, but if not, that they should be placed in the centre of the enclosure with the army drawn up around them. If parley with the Royalists did not produce acceptable conditions a threat could be made to blow up the whole train.

Meanwhile Essex placed his own regiment on the eastern side of Castle Dore, with Col. Butler's musketeers on the west of it towards Par, while Robartes and Col. Weare guarded the part towards Golant, which was the weakest point. They were faced by Grenville's Cornish foot and the horse under Lord Northampton. Driving up Roundhead stragglers was Capt. Brett who though wounded led a party of the King's men and beat the Roundheads from hedge to hedge. Charles, having accompanied his troops on this part of the campaign, knighted Brett on the spot for his bravery.

That busy day, Saturday, August 31, saw the harried Parliamentarians at bay, knowing fully what the end would be. Nevertheless at 6 o'clock that evening another stand was made, and a weak Parliament attack, which was driven off. As darkness came down the men of Weare's flank became disheartened and drifted away, and the defence owing to the weakness of the earthwork on that side, collapsed. On Sunday morning when daylight came Essex perceived that the end was only a matter of hours away. With Lord Robartes and one or two other officers he slipped back secretly into Fowey and from there, or from some small harbour such as Polkerris, went aboard a fishing boat and got safely to Plymouth, leaving the unfortunate Major-General Skippon to arrange a surrender.

Essex afterwards managed to put up a good defence for his flight, and persuaded Parliament to exonerate him. In fact he was later entrusted with further commands, and escaped all censure save that of history, although it is not certain what good a decision to stay with his men would have done.

Skippon called a Council of War on the Sunday morning, and suggested a breakthrough should be tried, but the men were too exhausted; the decision to surrender was made. A commission to arrange the terms of surrender met later that day, probably just below the ridge at Castle Dore where Lawhibbet farm stands today. The Royalist members of this commission were Prince Maurice and Lord Brentford, while the Roundheads had Philip Skippon, Christopher Whichcott and some others. The conditions agreed and granted were generous and open-handed showing that the Royalist commanders were not harsh to their defeated opponents. The same would not be said of the rank and file.

The Parliamentarians were to leave their 42 cannon and one

mortar, all their muskets and pikes, and all their carriages except one for each regiment. A wagon full of muskets and pikes was to be left behind, together with the remaining barrels of powder. The fit men, however, were to be allowed to march away to Poole and Wareham in Dorset with an escort to see them on the way. All officers above the rank of corporal were to keep their arms. The sick and wounded were to be conveyed to Fowey, and when recovered shipped to Plymouth. The colours were to be kept by their regiments.

So on Monday September 2 in the rain which had continued pitilessly the 'rebels' were marched away. In spite of the presence of the King, who had been with his men and slept under the hedges at night, the conditions of surrender were disobeyed by the Royalist soldiers. The Parliament men were robbed of their belongings. Royalist officers with drawn swords endeavoured to restrain them, but in vain. The Roundhead withdrawal was thus described—

> 'prest all of a heap like sheep—so dirty and dejected as was rare to see, none of them except some few of their officers that did look any of us in the face.'

Worse was to follow. When they reached Lostwithiel the inhabitants, who had been starved, plundered and their town and church despoiled during the Roundhead occupation stripped them even of their boots and clothing, covering them with bitter abuse and mockery. Of the six thousand who left Castle Dore, only one thousand ever reached Poole. The rest died of exhaustion, plague or were quietly murdered. A more fortunate few managed to find refuge in Plymouth.

King Charles said triumphantly to Francis Basset, Sheriff of Cornwall, on Wednesday, September 4, "Deare Mr Sheriffe, I leave Cornwall to you safe and sound". That may have been so, but the impoverished Cornish would have to contend with the aftermath of destruction and privation, and it would be many years before the ruin of war would be mended. Perhaps the terms of surrender, too, were too easy. Why, one may ask, were not the Parliament commanders taken prisoner, why were so many sent away to fight another day? One answer may lie in just this impoverishment of the Cornish, that there was little enough for the inhabitants alone, without the necessity of feeding many captive mouths. Perhaps, too, the shock of the siege and relief at its outcome may have given too optimistic a view of the progress of the war.

St. Bartholomew's, parish church of Lostwithiel, lost its roof when Parliament troops tried to smoke out Royalist prisoners who had escaped into the tower.

The font in St. Bartholomew's used to "christen" a horse by Parliamentarians during their occupation of Lostwithiel.

64

St. Nectan's chapel has never had its tower restored.

Certainly the town and countryside the victorious Cavaliers would survey was one devasted and ruined. The hamlet of Bridgend was a group of gutted cottages, and the fields around were trodden over by thousands of marching feet, showing no signs of harvestable growth. Cattle and sheep had disappeared, all having been taken for the use of the various armies. In the town itself the principal buildings all showed signs of damage, either deliberate vandalism or from the active bombardment from without. The church roof was blown off in a singular incident recorded in Symonds's diary. As well as using the church for stabling their Roundhead horses, Royalist prisoners were incarcerated there. The Provost-Marshal of the garrison had put several captives there the night they were to march away. Two of the prisoners got up into the tower of the church and shouted down in mockery of the retreating Parliamentarians. Unsuccessful in smoking them out by burning damp hay in the tower, or firing muskets up the interior, a barrel of powder was brought in and let off. This merely destroyed the roof without harming the prisoners.

Errata:- PICTURES on pages 65 & 72 are transposed.

Symonds also notes that while the church was used for stabling, the beautiful font was employed for watering the horses, and—

'in contempt of Christianity, Religion and the Church they brought a horse to the font, in the church, and there with their kind of ceremonies did as they called it christen the horse, and called him by the name Charles, in contempt of his sacred Majesty.'

As well as from its enemies, so also from its friends did the church receive hurt. A shot from the King's Redoubt on Beacon Hill damaged the steeple; it will be noticed that the fretted panel on that side of the octagonal lantern differs from the rest. This might indicate the seat of the damage.

During their sojourn in Lostwithiel the troops of Parliament numbering 10,000 vandalised the ancient Shire Hall, destroyed great quantities of Stannary, Exchequer and other records, as well as taking for their use the contents of shops, homes, and stores. In the hills east of the town, where the skirmishes had moved this way and that, there was damage to the ancient chapel of St Nectan. Its tall tower was battered down to the level of the church roof and the bells removed. A pinnacle and stones from the crown of the once-dignified tower lie in the churchyard, and there are others now in Boconnoc Park which probably came from St Nectan's.

Not long after the departure of the combatants a 'sickness' broke out, due no doubt to the starvation endured by the populace during the siege. The St Winnow registers record the burial of some ninety persons from the Bridgend area in the two months after September, about ten times the usual annual death-roll. No doubt the same sickness raged in the town, but there the registers are absent, as are the town records. They too, in all probability fell victim to the Roundhead fury.

At Menabilly the house was left as bare walls, entirely stripped. The estate was ruined, furniture, goods, cattle, woods, everything destroyed. In Fowey the same tale could be told, the town house of the Rashleighs in particular losing all its valuables and stores.

Before leaving Cornwall the King scattered knighthoods and titles around. He had already dubbed Capt. Brett a knight, in the field at Castle Dore, for his stalwart attacks on the Roundheads. He now made Francis Basset a knight, a well-deserved honour since he had served his sovereign with energy and self-sacrifice. It was he who organised the privateers who brought such rich prizes into

Cornish ports, and he had spent some £1,500 of his own money on the defences of St Michael's Mount. John Arundell of Lanherne and Charles Trevanion of Caerhayes were also knighted, and Sir Richard Vyvyan was made a baronet. Sir Richard Grenville was given all the lands of Lord Robartes at Lanhydrock, and also those of Sir Francis Drake at Buckland Abbey; this descendant of the more famous Sir Francis was a supporter of the Parliament cause.

Flushed with euphoria after the success of the Lostwithiel affair, the King now moved against Plymouth. On September 10 his army of some fifteen thousand soldiers advanced from Roborough and poured down the hills towards what are now Compton and Mannamead within the city border. Twenty-eight guns began replying to the Roundhead cannon which had opened up from the Maudlyn Work on North Hill. Charles then called on the town to surrender, only to receive the laconic and determined reply—"Never". Lord Robartes was now the Governor of Plymouth and his presence and the challenge of the King stiffened the resistance of the townsfolk once again.

Ranged against the large Royalist army however was only a small garrison so far as numbers were concerned. Luckily reinforcements came in from the remnants of Essex's army, and from ships in the Cattewater, whose crews gave their assistance to the townsfolk. Nevertheless with this help there were still only 150 guns, 2,500 foot and 400 horse for the defence of four miles of line and stockade.

Surprisingly Charles made only one serious attack, and this was not successful. It was directed towards the western end of the defence line from Stonehouse to Pennycomequick, but his troops were repulsed with heavy losses. This was a severe setback to the Royalist cause. The Lostwithiel victory, which Essex described as 'the greatest blow we have ever suffered', had greatly strengthened the King's position and would have enabled him to recover his losses in the North, if, as the French ambassador said 'he knows how to use the victory'. But its use was thwarted or thrown away in the vain effort at Pennycomequick.

During Charles's stay near Plymouth he used Widey Court as his headquarters, and every morning came out with his guards to promenade on the slopes of Mannamead. The firing of guns and the military posturing aroused the mockery of the townsfolk, who nicknamed the declivity 'Vaporing Hill'; the name 'Vapron Road' in that district preserves the memory.

The failure of the King's attack marked the end of serious threat to Plymouth. He and Prince Maurice marched away, leaving Sir Richard Grenville in charge of the blockade, which died down during the autumn into a series of sporadic incidents in which neither side gained advantage though Grenville took Saltash, exacting brutal reprisals for its obdurate resistance in October 1644.

The new year, however, brought a fresh danger. Grenville mounted a strong attack at four points along the line of defence, from Pennycomequick eastward, in January, 1645. Only at one outwork did he have temporary success, but there too his soldiers were soon afterwards counter-attacked with total loss. One more attempt, in February at Mount Stamford also failed. It was the beginning of the end for Grenville. The year 1645 would see the complete overturning of the Royalist cause. Plymouth could begin to lower its guard, until in the following year the triumphant Fairfax in command of the renewed Roundhead army would move into Devon and the threat to the town would disappear. The inhabitants lived under seige and blockade from November 1642 until February, 1646 when the ordeal was finally over. Eight thousand died in Plymouth defending it, trade was at a standstill and there was much privation. But no other besieged town in the west could boast as Plymouth could—that it had remained in its original allegiance since the outbreak of the war.

In this spring of 1645 the King's son, the Prince of Wales, the future Charles II, was made Commander of the western army. He was only fifteen years old at the time, and was advised by a Council among whose members were Edward Hyde and Ralph Hopton. One of the difficulties facing the command in the west was the continual jousting between incompatible officers, such as the dissolute Goring and the savage, bullying Richard Grenville. This lack of co-operation cost the Royalists the town of Taunton, which might have been gained by a combined attack pressed home. But the time for Cavalier gains was rapidly passing in the face of a new threat.

The counties of East Anglia had long worked together in harmony for local defence in the Parliament cause, in which the region was united. Under skilful leadership this Association army was turning into an efficient and aggressive force in which Oliver Cromwell was becoming a prominent and respected officer. The principal Parliament army found itself increasingly challenged by the swift rise of the Eastern Association army, especially as among fighting men everywhere on that side radical political and religious ideas were becoming popular. Many were asking if the old leaders were sufficiently in control, would the army be better if it were unified, and would it be to its advantage if it were freed from the involvement of its commanders in Parliamentary lobbying and interference?

The failure of Essex at Lostwithiel was another cause for serious heart-searching, adding another weight to the side of reform. In 1644 Parliament passed a Self-denying Ordinance, whereby those in army command relinquished their seats in the Commons, thus opening the way at one stroke to the necessary reorganising of their force, but also to the loosening of control by Parliament, in whose cause it was supposedly fighting. With the forcefulness of such men as Fairfax and Cromwell the New Model Army, with unified and efficient command by soldiers who knew their job, was formed. Not a little of the impetus for it came from disillusionment after Essex's Lostwithiel surrender.

The effect of the New Model Army's efficiency was felt at the battle of Naseby, when on June 4, 1645 the Roundhead army, with Fairfax as General and Cromwell as Lieutenant, and with a superiority on their part of two to one in infantry and even more in cavalry, the Royalists were routed and scattered. It was clear the King's cause was broken. Individual battles might be won by him, but the war was clearly lost as a whole. Fairfax then turned his attention to the westcountry. Early in July he was at Dorchester, and taking advantage of the estrangement between Goring and Grenville he occupied Yeovil and then Bridgwater. This latter town was a Royalist arsenal, and great stores of war material were seized. Establishing his position before attempting to move into Cornwall, Fairfax stormed Bristol, where Prince Rupert surrendered all too speedily, to the great distress of the King who had expected him to make a stand. Here again immense quantities of ammunition, arms, and military stores fell to Fairfax.

The inexorable advance continued. By October 1645 Fairfax's army was at Tiverton. Here he heard of an insurrection against the King at St Ives, put down with harsh severity by Richard Grenville, but it was evidence of coming collapse even in loyal Cornwall. In Royalist concern for the safety of the Prince of Wales he and his Council were moved to Launceston from Bristol but even there danger threatened. At Bodmin Hopton's and Hyde's appeals to the

Cornish to rise in support of the King fell on deaf ears. The Cornish, who had suffered so much loss, were tired of the war, impoverished and sorely disillusioned by the quarrelling of the commanders. The high hope and spirit of the first colourful days under Sir Bevil and his companions had quite vanished away.

Before long Fairfax, with a crushing defeat of Hopton at Torrington in February 1646, swept all the Royalists out of Devonshire. Some found refuge in Cornwall. The Prince of Wales and his retinue moved to the safety of Pendennis Castle, while around them the Cornish Cavaliers fell into even greater disorder and pathetic disunity. The unfortunate Hopton was made supreme commander in the west, a most thankless task. But under him, had there been greater unanimity among the Royalist leaders even then a base might have been preserved for the King in Cornwall. As his subordinates Richard Grenville was made General of foot, and Lord Wentworth General of the horse. But the evil genius which ever moved Grenville had put him at odds with Hopton and he refused to serve under him as an inferior. It was gross insubordination. The Prince of Wales was compelled to arrest Richard Grenville and at his order he was confined in St Michael's Mount. Yet still the old Grenville glamour remained. He still had some 'pull' with the Cornish, who demanded his immediate release, overlooking his cruelty and his disobedience of the Prince's orders. The Cornish army was sullen and resentful at the refusal to release Richard.

It was fortunate indeed for the westcountry that the General of the advancing Roundhead army was the great Fairfax, a Yorkshireman of moderation, straightforward and generous. It was he who preserved the Minster from Puritan vandalism when the city of York fell to the Parliamentarians. To each Cornishman taken prisoner in his Devon campaigns he gave two shillings and his freedom. He sent his chaplain, the fanatical preacher Hugh Peters, in unwontedly conciliatory vein to soften up the Royalist gentry of east Cornwall to obtain their help in keeping the area quiet during the Roundhead advance. By these diplomatic tactics this advance was greatly facilitated.

Fairfax entered Bodmin on March 2, and his army camped that night at Castle-an-dinas on the Goss Moor. At this point Edward Hyde and other companions of the Prince of Wales left with him to sail to the Isles of Scilly, their contingent being much plundered by the sailors under their Dutch captain on the way. Unwillingly, relentlessly pushed back to Truro, commanding a weary, demoralised army eager to surrender, surrounded by a population ready to welcome the invader, Hopton was obliged to treat for terms. At Tresillian Bridge, a few miles east of Truro, the Royalist army laid down its arms on March 12. Hopton immediately left to join his Prince on the Scillies. Some days afterwards two forts in the Falmouth harbour, St Mawes Castle, and the Dennis Fort at the mouth of the Helford river, which Sir Richard Vyvyan had built and maintained out of his own pocket, gave in. Only Pendennis and the Mount held out for the King. The latter surrendered on April 16, at which point the Prince of Wales with three hundred refugees sailed for Jersey en route for France and exile.

But Pendennis held on. Under old John Arundell, who was seventy years old or more the garrison of about a thousand fought off attacks and endured increasing privations. On land a siege was imposed by Col. Hammond and Col. Fortescue, and at sea Capt. Batten and a flotilla of ships prevented the entry of supplies. Soon the horses, themselves starving, had to be slaughtered to feed the inhabitants of the isolated Castle. When the surrender of the Castle was demanded in the name of Fairfax and the Parliament, the septuagenarian commander nicknamed 'Jack-for-the-King' Arundell returned this spirited reply—

'Sir,

The Castle was committed to my government by His Majesty, who by our laws hath the command of the Castles and Forts of this Kingdom, and my age of seventy summons me hence shortly. Yet I shall desire no other testimony to follow my departure than my conscience to God and loyalty to His Majesty, whereto I am bound by all the obligations of nature, duty and oath. I wonder you demand the Castle without authority from His Majesty, which if I should render, I brand myself and my posterity with the indelible character of Treason. And having taken less than two minutes resolution, I resolve that I will here bury myself before I deliver up this Castle to such as fight against His Majesty and that nothing you can threaten is formidable to me in respect of the loss of loyalty and conscience.

Your servant,

John Arundell of Trerice.

As time went on however the condition of the garrison worsened and it was obvious that, gallantry notwithstanding, surrender must be accepted. But Pendennis nevertheless held out until August 17, for five months of starvation and disheartenment as news of defeat after defeat for the Royalists came in. Their King was by then a prisoner of the Scots, the Prince of Wales and his advisors exiles in France.

The terms granted to the garrison were generous since its spirit was admired by friend and foe alike. The survivors, some 24 officers and 900 men marched out homewards, with 'colours flying, trumpets sounding, drums beating, match lighted at both ends, bullets in their mouths, and to every soldier twelve charges of powder'. Many of the men died soon afterwards as a result of their privation. John Arundell marched out with the rest, his heart heavy. But his hopes would be as inextinguishable as his loyalty.

The Civil War in Cornwall could have had a no more fitting end.

Pendennis Castle, Falmouth. Last mainland outpost held by the Royalists. When finally driven to surrender their courage was acknowledged by General Fairfax who allowed them to march out with colours flying.

CHAPTER 5

Plots and Skirmishes

After the cessation of hostilities came the reckoning. It was clear that those who had actively supported the Royalist cause and given help to it would be penalised. There were several prominent Cornishmen who could not bring themselves to submit to Parliament rule and reprisal, and who therefore followed the Prince into exile in France. These refugees included the Governor of the Isles of Scilly Sir Francis Godolphin; Bevil's son, Sir John; and Sir Henry Killigrew, who died only a few months after joining the exiles. The little court was speedily reduced almost to penury, but their lot was not much worse than that of those who remained in Cornwall.

In addition to having given generously in support of the King's cause, and having their goods spoiled or requisitioned by one side or another, and sometimes both, now there were heavy fines to pay to compound for the retaining of their estates, a sixth, or even up to a half of the value. Jonathan Rashleigh, one of the collectors for His Majesty's Mint, had given generously of his wealth and seen his house and lands ruined at a cost of £10,300; now he had a fine of £1,085 to pay. John Arundell was assessed at £10,000; Lord Mohun £2,000; Thomas Lower of St Winnow £1,174; Sir John Trelawny £647, and Sir Richard Vyvyan £600. This last would have been assessed at much more, save for the intercession of Fairfax, who also obtained concessions for the eastern Cornish Royalist gentry who had co-operated with him after surrendering. The Bassets of the Mount were so impoverished that they had to sell out to the Parliamentary Sir John St Aubyn in 1657, and there were many such transactions on a smaller scale throughout the succeeding years. It would be difficult to express in terms of modern monetary value the losses and fines.

The arrangements for sequestrations and compounding for Royalist estates were handled by the County Committee, set up in each county in 1642, but for obvious reasons inoperative in Cornwall until 1646. The composition of the Cornish Committee was similar to that of any competent body of the time, the Royalists may have had to be ruled, but it was by their own equals. The Committee was not composed of landless revolutionaries, as might be today, but of county gentry and others of standing. The sphere of action entrusted to the County Committee included the keeping of order, maintaining defences and garrisons, the sequestration of delinquents' (i.e. Royalists') property, collection of the weekly assessments and the excise. One new feature arose from this last matter—the collectors were a paid company of agents and factors, and for the first time in the country a bureaucracy appeared; the Civil War brought this as well as poverty. While under the monarchy direct tax had been intermittent, now under Parliament it was to be a continuous feature of life.

Next to suffer were the parish clergy, many of whom had been ardent supporters of the King, to whom they had sworn allegiance. The Parliament and the army, however much they might differ over the religious arrangements they wanted in England, agreed on one thing—it would be neither that of the Anglican or Roman Churches. Episcopacy had been abolished, now the Prayer-book was forbidden. Clergy who would not subscribe to the Parliament laws in Church matters were turned out of their livings and their homes. A small pittance was allotted to them out of the parish stipend, but this was often left unpaid or diminished arbitrarily. About seventy of the Cornish clergy were 'outed' from their parishes. Some found a refuge in the local 'big house' as tutors or stewards, some earned a living through medicine or the law, but many existed on a level just above starvation.

Hugh Colmer, rector of Ladock, was reduced to destitution, so his parishioners sent him their children to educate until even this was forbidden by law. Richard Tucker had eight small children and was a widower. Neighbours sheltered him and his family for a time. Thomas Flavell, vicar of Mullion, had been an outspoken man in the King's support, and was searched for with the intention of hanging him. When the scare was over, during which he had hidden himself, he was allowed to live in the parsonage, but without any income. He vowed he would not cut his beard until the King came back, and he kept his promise, too.

Service in the churches was performed by some Puritan cleric or even at times by unlettered laymen. A few, very few, of the Cornish clergy were prepared to submit to Parliament, and carry out duties in several parishes to supply some sort of devotion for the people, even to using the Prayer-book forms by memory. There were on the other hand several sincerely convinced Puritan clergy who had all along fully supported the reforms made by Parliament in the affairs of the Church. Among these were Charles Morton of Blisland, John Wills of Morval, Jaspar Hicks of Landrake, and Thomas Peters of Mylor, brother of Hugh, chaplain to Cromwell. These and others would be 'outed' in their turn at the Restoration, being unable to accept the Anglican system, and forming a nucleus of what would be nonconformity in later years. They were mostly moderate presbyterians and Parliament men.

The ascendancy of the Commons reached out to the churches themselves, and under the instructions of the County Committee much destruction was wrought, and things which had survived the earlier storm of the sixteenth century now fell to the Puritan axe. Thus, the rood-screen at St Ives, together with the organ were taken down at the order of the Committee and the cost of £1. 15s. 7d. appears recorded in the town account. Stained windows were smashed, altars removed, paintings scrubbed out or whitewashed, communion rails broken up. Common board trestle tables were employed for the infrequent communion services, and all music, save that of the metrical psalms forbidden. The estates of the bishop and dean, the cathedral chapter and college property and that belonging to ancient foundations were confiscated. Strict discipline over morals and Sunday observance was imposed. Christmas was abolished, and all church festivals and jollifications like church ales had to be abandoned.

Parliament moved still further against the traditional order of the Church of England in 1653, when another ordinance was passed requiring marriage before a Justice of the Peace. Lay Registrars of births and deaths were appointed. In Truro John Bagwell was Registrar and the first civil marriage following his installation in November, 1653, was between Richard Garland of St Veep and Mary Bramshaw of Veryan. In the register of St Mary's, Launceston, there is the comment—'27 Nov. 1655 Hereafter follow marriages by laymen, according to the profaneness and giddyness of the times, without precedent or example in any Christian Kingdom or Commonwealth from the birth of Christ unto this very year 1655'.

The end of the war in 1646 had been followed by bad harvests, mines were flooded, bridges remained unmended. As a result of malnutrition plague spread in the western parts, stemming from Pendennis and reaching to neighbouring towns. St Ives had to be isolated, food being placed at the parish borders by sympathetic people from outside. In spite of this, five hundred townsfolk died. Within a couple of years of the ending of the war there was rapidly increasing discontent, fuel for another outbreak of conflict.

Meanwhile the King had been playing off the Scots, the army, and Parliament against each other. Charles was, it must be remembered, a Stuart, and King also of Scotland, however much disliked or rejected. As time went on the growth of political and religious radicalism in the army brought it into collision with Parliament, which was itself increasingly divided between the old moderates who wanted an accommodation with the King, and the new race of Independents, Levellers, Fifth-Monarchy men and other sectaries.

With the passing months the memory of the King's exactions and misrule faded, and his claim to have stood for the known and tried old laws seemed more credible in view of the unpopularity of the County Committees with their endless meddling, and the harsh realities of Parliamentary government. Many hitherto committed to the popular cause found themselves increasingly isolated and became neutrals or opponents of the new order. Among these last was Lord Robartes himself who became dissatisfied with Cromwell's policies. He returned to Lanhydrock after the relief of Plymouth, employing his time in improving his estate. The avenue of sycamores, some few of which survive, was planted by him in 1648, and the gatehouse, begun in the 1630s, was completed during this period. He survived to see the Restoration, and was received into favour by the new King.

There were many who could not content themselves with planting avenues of sycamores, but were goaded by the increasingly harsh conditions, and the mounting taxation to support extravagant naval and military establishments, to take up arms again.

In March, 1648 the Parliamentary commander of Pembroke Castle in Wales refused to hand over to his relief, and declared for the King. Most of south Wales joined in. The counties of Essex and Kent largely declared for Charles. Soon the Scots were over the border, and a great part of the navy took the Royalist side. Everywhere there were people ready to help overthrow an unpopular government if it appeared to totter. London itself was in danger.

Fairfax sent Cromwell off to deal with Pembroke Castle and

Wales, and with orders then to proceed north to meet the challenge of Scots and English. After some delay in reducing Pembroke Cromwell achieved a decisive victory over the considerable Royalist and Scots force at Preston. Another principal action of this 'Second Civil War' was the siege of Colchester, which resisted for several weeks during which the garrison, townsfolk, women and children were reduced to appalling conditions of near starvation. Uncharacteristically Fairfax refused to allow the women and children to withdraw through the Parliamentary lines. This harshness was long remembered with bitterness.

Obviously the risk of trouble in Cornwall was high, with its Royalist sympathies, its seething discontent and its accessibility to France and to agents of the Prince of Wales who were always coming and going. Parliament sent Sir Hardress Waller with a strong force into the west to preserve order and to quell any sign of rebellion. The County Committee travelled here and there in Cornwall with the same intention. The Sheriff of Cornwall reported that several 'malignant gentlemen' were planning to disturb the peace, and Waller ordered the arrest of Sir John Trelawny, his son Jonathan, and Robert Harris, who had been earlier in charge of the King's troops around Plymouth.

Hints of local trouble came from a Penzance shopkeeper, one Gubbs, who had fallen foul of Richard Grenville, but the County Committee led by John Moyle found all quiet at Helston on their visit there. They left on their journey to Launceston on May 16. Their departure appears to have set off the powder keg. That night an insurrection broke out at Helston, and 200 Royalists gathered on open ground between Penzance and Gulval. The leaders of these local 'rebels' were men of minor rank, such as Major Grosse of St Buryan, William Keigwin of Mousehole, Capt. Maddern of Penzance, Capt. Tresilian of St Erth, and some others. Behind these men, who carried little weight, it was suspected there were others, notably John Arundell of Trerice, who was supposed to be ringleader and author of the plan to rise. There was immediate alarm, as shortly there was plundering and looting in Penzance, shopkeeper Gubbs being a prime target since he refused to contribute to the Royalist 'rebels' cause. However by Saturday 20th, the Sheriff got to Helston with reinforcements and proceeded to Breage with 400 horse and 120 foot troopers. By the Monday Penzance was taken, with light casualties on the attacking side and the loss of 60 or 70 Royalists.

But the rising was not over. A couple of days later the Helston folk heard that Mullion was up, with 120 'rebels', which put them into great fright. Making a round tour the Mullion men moved over Goonhilly Down to St Keverne, and on to Mawgan, having in their progress collected 300 foot and 40 horse from farms and villages of the Meneage district. At this the Helston mayor took alarm, since it appeared that these latest 'rebels' would be in the town before reinforcements could arrive from Penzance. Collecting a few local Parliamentarians and a few horses he finally met the relieving troops from Penzance in the evening of 23 May. Led by the mayor of Helston they advanced towards Mawgan, and met the 'rebels' in the open space in front of the village church. There was spirited fighting for a short time, but the 'rebels' retreated into the ancient earthwork called the 'Gear', near Trelowarren overlooking the Helford river. There was a general stampede as they were driven from their position. Soon the district was full of fleeing Royalists, of whom some made their way to St Keverne, and, joining hands, leaped down into the sea in their despair; others hid in old tin workings, caves, and any handy shelter.

This incident is remembered as the 'Gear Rout', the Cornish insurrection of 1648. The danger had been considerable to the Parliament side, although the numbers involved were small. The House of Commons took it very seriously, thanking Waller, St Aubyn, and other Cornish gentry who had quelled the revolt. Some of the chief Cornish Royalists, who were all in one way or another involved, were arrested and detained for a while until things settled down.

Compared with the large campaigns of the earlier war this was a small and pathetic affair affecting only the Mount's Bay area and the Lizard, but it was followed later in the year 1648 by a much more serious incident, in which the Isles of Scilly were seized and held for the King. The Isles formed a useful outpost from which to harry the Channel trade and pin down Parliament naval forces, but they were hardly the most comfortable spot to settle on, being at that time bleak and desolate, the haunt of smugglers and criminals. Nearly all supplies had to be brought in by sea. There, however, Sir John Grenville, aided by Prince Rupert who commanded a mixed group of vessels prowling and pouncing on Parliament ships, established a fortified haven for privateers which damaged the Channel trade for the next three years. Rupert and the remnant of the fleet which remained loyal to the King kept the Isles supplied, and the whole affair became a great nuisance to the government. It was, in comparison with earlier battles, a mere pinprick, but with many other symptoms of continuing sympathy and support for the King, it kept Parliament constantly on the alert.

The triumph of the Roundhead army was however complete on the mainland. The recent outbreaks being now efficiently quelled, Parliament found itself dominated by army rule. The moderate Presbyterian members were excluded from the remains of the Long Parliament, which was reduced to a mere sixty Independent members under the influence of the army. Among the survivors of 'Pryde's Purge', which thus confined the Commons to a mere 'Rump' were the Cornish members Francis Rous of St Dominic and John Carew, half-brother to the unfortunate Sir Alexander. The former, Rous, perhaps deserves mention as the author of the words of that metrical psalm we sing to the tune *'Crimond'*.

The Rump now turned its attention to the King, held in captivity. A Commission was appointed to try him for treason and crime against the people. John Carew was one of the judges. But by what right and authority and law was the fount of power, the King, judged by those who were his subjects? That fiery preacher, Hugh Peters, of the Fowey family, who had so effectively spurred on Roundhead armies with his Old Testament harangues, in sermon after sermon incited the Commission to find the King guilty. On January 30, 1649 King Charles walked calmly to the block at Whitehall, his execution arousing a deep groan from the people present and converting many as friends to his cause who were hitherto enemies.

England was now a Commonwealth. The lawful King, Charles II, an exile in France, but ever eager to support any blow for his return, had much professed support from the French ruler and his mother the Queen Henrietta Maria. Charles was proclaimed King in Scotland, and this was repeated in France and on the Scillies. The Royal cause now had its martyr in the executed King, and the faithful were stirred to grief and further discontent, the more determined to support the new sovereign.

A Royalist agent, one Col. Keane, reported to the King that Sir John Arundell of Lanherne and Col. Richard Arundell, who had served under Sir Richard Grenville, were asking that Sir Richard should be sent to the Scillies from France with a force of 1,000 infantry, 300 horses and 40 barrels of powder. When this would be done, then the Arundells would rise with a considerable armed force, but it was an essential condition that Sir Richard Grenville himself should appear in Cornwall. Charles promised that the hoped-for arms and munitions would be sent to the islands and suggested that Royalists of note in other westcountry counties should be alerted, while some strongholds such as Pendennis might be seized. It was rumoured in June 1650 that Hopton, Grenville and others of influence in the cause were gathered in the Scillies making preparations.

The government took alarm and set in motion precautionary moves. Troops were moved into the west, and Cornish leaders were arrested and imprisoned, among them Francis Godolphin, Sir Charles Trevanion, John Arundell of Trerice, and Sir Nicholas Prideaux. The rank and file, meanwhile, were awaiting a landing force from the Isles before they committed themselves. Charles was unable to carry out his part of the plan. The French promises and their actions were two quite different things and no supporting army came from there. The Westminster government once more had the upper hand, although the reality was that Cromwell governed now with the army, using the Rump as a front. The Duchy of Cornwall was abolished, as there was no Duke and no Lords. All Royal estates were put up for sale, finding in fact few and hesitating buyers, who feared the effects of a reversal of things. The King's collections of pictures and other items of value assembled with such discrimination were dispersed and sold.

In March 1651 a Dutch fleet under van Tromp was sent by the Netherlands government to turn out the Scilly privateers, who were such a nuisance to ships in that area, demanding reparation for the damage done to the Dutch sea trade. It is said that there was a secret order to treat with Sir John Grenville for the surrender of the Isles to the Dutch government, which of course was contemptuously refused. But hearing of the Dutch presence the English government sent Admiral Blake to attend to the matter and reclaim the Scillies. Blake's force landed on Tresco in May and set about the bombardment of the principal island, St Mary's where Sir John Grenville had his garrison consisting of 800 men. On Tresco, where some of the buildings of this period remain, Blake found and captured 25 pieces of ordnance and 116 prisoners. Twenty of the Royalist defenders were killed, and forty drowned. At the same time a vessel taking refugees to France was seized.

After a while the garrison on St Mary's capitulated. On that island there were 50 barrels of powder, abundance of great shot and much ordnance, while a French vessel coming in with supplies was surprised and taken. Sir John Grenville extricated himself from the collapse of this last venture and joined Charles II again at his court on the continent. His influence there would be crucial in the future.

The prospect of any further rising in Cornwall was extinguished when Cromwell took the powers of a dictator, assuming the title of Lord Protector. This evoked the disgust of Fifth-Monarchy men, among them John Carew, Alexander's half-brother. These sectaries looked to Christ as the true new monarch, and feared that Cromwell would soon 'King it'. Oliver dismissed his elected Parliament-in-part, the Rump, and its hand-picked successor, ruling at last with the help of Major-Generals, each set over a part of the country with an army paid for by taxes on the Royalists. It was naked military rule, and more despotic than Charles I had ever dreamed of. Yet, quite paradoxically, this period transformed the standing of this country in Europe.

In September 1658 the feared Oliver Cromwell died. His son, Richard, who succeeded him, was not of a calibre sufficient to carry the burden of rule. So this 'Tumbledown Dick' as he was nicknamed, was soon swept aside, and the country fell completely into the hands of the Major-Generals.

The most influential among these was George Monck, in command of the army in Scotland. He had growing hopes for the renewal of Parliament, whose side he had early supported. Monck was a Devon man, and a cousin of the Grenvilles. His clerical brother Nicholas had been appointed to the Kilkhampton living by Sir John Grenville anticipating the contact might be useful one day. That day was arriving.

In July 1659 Sir John knowing the mind of Charles II from his attendance on him at his court in exile, sent Parson Monck into Scotland with instructions to try to persuade the General to come out and declare himself as a supporter of a truly free and elected Parliament and for the King's return. Monck not unnaturally took some time to prepare himself and his colleagues for this momentous step. In the following January, 1660 he marched with his army into

England, persuading or forcing the other Generals to a like mind, finding in all but a few cases little opposition. In London Monck met Sir John Grenville, and passed to him terms on which the King's return might be acceptable to the country.

Grenville returned from the court in France with letters from the King. A newly-elected Parliament had reassembled in its old full form, the excluded members being admitted. On May 1 the King's letter was read to the House of Commons which publicly thanked Sir John Grenville, described by Pepys in his diary as 'Grenville, one of the bedchamber to the King', for bringing the letter from Charles.

So it was that on May 25, 1660, there stepped from a ship at Dover a tall, swarthy man, distinctly French in appearance rather than English, amid the acclamations of the huge crowd of notables and bystanders. His Majesty, Charles II, King of England, had come home to his people. Few would greet him more wholeheartedly than those who had never wavered from their allegiance in loyal Cornwall, in which so much blood had been shed for the Royal cause.

CHAPTER 6

What Remains?

The noise and destruction of the Civil War have long since passed into the history books, and have been overlaid by the fiercer sounds of more recent and wider wars. Indeed, so far forgotten are the battles in which the names of Grenville, Hopton, Essex and Fairfax resounded that even those who live on or near the sites of past warfare may not be clear as to what really happened in their own neighbourhood, and what was the significance of it. There are many half-understood traditions and tales about the Civil War, but except by a few students the actual progress of events is often not known. It is hoped that this book may have helped the reader to a better realisation of the motives as to why his forefathers entered on 'this war without an enemy', as the Parliamentarian Sir William Waller described it to his friend but opponent Sir Ralph Hopton, and what ensued from the struggle. We ask then, What Remains?

Every schoolboy will know that as a result of the Civil War and the Restoration of the monarchy in 1660 a great step forward was made to the present system of constitutional monarchy, with effective rule vested in the Commons. The seventeenth century saw a great shift of power away from the sovereign to Parliament, and that remains. The present-day balance has been built up piece by piece, but the Civil War provided the foundation.

This book however does not purport to be a political treatise. On those matters the reader will have his own opinions. But the Civil War as a fact of history must be taken into account. It cannot be ignored, nor what it gained and lost cast aside as unimportant.

Apart then from the abstract political and historical results of the war, we may ask ourselves, what remains? What can still be seen to bring back the memory, jog the imagination?

At Bradock Down the site of the battle is now in Boconnoc Park, which was enclosed at the beginning of the nineteenth century and planted with trees. The Park is open to the public occasionally. Entering by the gate on the south side of Bradock Church the surrounding flat area is the spot at which the Parliament troops under Col. Ruthven were drawn up, facing south down the hill. The obelisk on the opposite hill has nothing to do with the battle, being of later erection in a different context. But it stands in what was probably a shallow redoubt, as that is the locality where the Royalist forces were gathered under Sir Bevil Grenville and Sir Ralph Hopton. The line of the drive is very roughly an indication of the direction of the Royalist advance on that memorable Thursday, January 19, 1643, when the first of the Cornish Royalist victories of any importance was obtained. There is no monument to the actual battle, nor has any quantity of relics been found. There is, however, near the Bodmin Lodge, on the main road from Lostwithiel to Liskeard, a memorial erected in 1846, consisting of an ancient granite cross on an inappropriately tall plinth with an inscription marking both the primeval supposed 'Druid idolatry' and civil bloodshed. While all the area featured in the battles of 1643 and 1644 there is no particular known signficance in this actual spot. The general locality might be that at which the Struggle by Challenge took place. Local tradition says that some of the tumuli or barrows on the Downs might be the place where the dead were buried, as with few exceptions they would not have been buried in the parish churchyards at that time.

Near Stratton the hill around which the battle was fought can be reached from the road from Stratton to Bideford. There is a monument on the site, and the old manor house, which is now the Tree Inn, bears a plaque commemorating the fact that this was the headquarters of Hopton and other leaders at the time. There are preserved there some old scythes, said to be part of the improvised weaponry at this early battle. In the parish church there is a small display of relics. The anniversary of the battle—May 16—is still a day of festivity at Stratton.

The home of the Grenvilles at Stowe, in these northerly parts, is no more. The great house which replaced the older mansion at the triumph of Sir John after the Restoration to accord with his magnificent titles has gone. The terraces and gardens can just be traced.

In the Lostwithiel district the countryside remains to display the tactics of the siege, and there are many buildings and features to remind us of it. Lanhydrock House, the residence of Lord Robartes, once taken and possessed by Richard Grenville and in which Robartes's children were confined while their father was Governor of Plymouth, is open to the public in the summer. Respryn Bridge,

Restormel Castle, Lostwithiel bridge, the Shire Hall, or Duchy Palace, and the parish church are all of interest. In this last building is the beautiful font, at which the Roundheads 'christened' a horse, and the signs of an earlier roof can be discerned on the tower wall. The King's Redoubt, on Beacon Hill, from which a shot damaged the church, is on private land. It is difficult to find, being surrounded by nineteenth-century mine workings and is filled with brambles.

St Nectan's chapel, between Lostwithiel and Boconnoc still lacks the top stages of its tower, the stump having been roughly tidied up about 1680. Stones from its crown are still in the churchyard. At Cliff in the parish of St Veep the cottage by the beach has two cannon balls built in over the windows, which were probably fired from the Golant side of the river in the last desperate attempt to force a crossing before the Parliament surrender in August, 1644. In the Lostwithiel Museum there are a few relics, and some more exist in private hands.

Down south on the east side of the river Fowey stands Hall, now a farm, which was seized for the King by Sir Jacob Astley, and nearby Hall Walk in which Charles narrowly escaped being killed by a shot across the river from the town. Below is Polruan fort, also fortified to prevent supply vessels from entering the harbour.

Further west in Cornwall Pendennis Castle still presides over the wide harbour at Falmouth and reminds one of the brave stand made by 'Jack-for-the-King' Arundell. This was the last outpost on the mainland of Cornwall to hold out for the King. In Falmouth the parish church of King Charles the Martyr was founded by Sir Peter Killigrew and others in 1662 as a memorial of the Civil War and as a reassertion of the Royal supremacy in the full tide of pious sentiment over the significance of the death of Charles I. The Dennis Fort, on the Helford estuary, can just be traced on the headland on the west side of the Carrick Roads.

A few miles east of Truro is Tresillian, where at the bridge in March 1646 the Royalist troops laid down their arms at the surrender by Hopton to Fairfax. There is a tablet on one of the buildings newly placed to commemorate this event.

In Plymouth almost nothing remains to remind the visitor of the gallant resistance of the townsfolk during the long siege and blockade. The land where the fiercest skirmishes took place has long since been built over. Widey Court was demolished many years ago.

Only the names of 'Vapron Road', in Mannamead, and 'Prince Maurice Road' in Laira remind us of the days when King and Prince were present at the siege. The familiar name 'Freedom Fields' signifies to most people now the great hospital there rather than the Plymouth and Parliament victory in the 'Sabbath Day Fight' of December, 1643. Freedom Park, laid out in Victorian times, seems rather to weaken and emasculate the remembrance of the event it commemorates. Open fields would be a better reminder. There is a memorial there to the battle, at which the late Isaac Foot, a great Cromwellian, was wont to lay a wreath in remembrance of the victory on the anniversary. Odd cannon balls and bullets have turned up from time to time, and occasionally the skeleton of a defender buried where he fell.

The massive Citadel on the Hoe, which replaces the smaller earlier fort and the Castle was built at the order of Charles II and commenced in 1666, ostensibly to defend the harbour. It was, and is, immediately obvious that many of the gun ports are placed so as to dominate the town also. Charles was making sure that the Plymouthians would never again rebel against the monarchy!

As one examines these things, rusting now and silent, the imagination awakens to the time when they were handled in anger by the men of one side or the other in a vigour now vanished. They took part in a conflict which involved the whole country, and in which courage, chivalry, and even in a strange way, romance, attended the first years of the struggle in Cornwall.

As one might stir the pot-pourri in an ancient mansion a fragrance arises at the remembrance of the personal character and enterprise of the great Grenville family. So much of the story of the Civil War in Cornwall is a Grenville story. Their name rings through the western campaigns and echoes in the Restoration itself. Sir Bevil, gentle, home-loving, mildly devout, but when the call came by so much the first to raise his own standard for the King, and to rally his friends, his tenants, his servants successfully to arms. His influence, with that of Ralph Hopton, was paramount in the welding of the Cornish militia into a powerful and feared fighting machine, at the same time one devout and in victory merciful. Sir Bevil gave his loyalty, his prosperity and at the last, so grievously for the Cornish, his life for the King in a manner movingly pure and unselfish.

Nor did his brother Sir Richard, harshly wrought into a stern fighting man in the bitter Thirty Years' War on the continent forfeit the respect of his countrymen. When in the necessity caused by this Grenville's disobedience of his orders the Prince of Wales was obliged to arrest him and detain him on the Mount, the Cornishmen clamoured for his immediate release. He too was a Cornishman, but above all he was a Grenville. Neither was there any hope at all of a Cornish rising in 1650 unless the requirement of his presence in the county could be met. Of all the Grenvilles, Richard's end was the most miserable. Embittered and forbidden access to the court of Charles II while he was in exile, owing to his accusation of treachery on the part of Edward Hyde and others whom he disliked, Richard died in 1659, just before the Restoration, in Ghent. It is said there was a stone on his grave with the words, 'Sir Richard Grenville, the King's General in the West'. The stone and the grave cannot now be traced.

Sir John Grenville, no less in stature than his father Sir Bevil brightens the later actions of the war. Placed on his father's horse at Lansdowne by faithful Anthony Payne when Sir Bevil was felled during battle, John's presence rallied the faltering Cornish, although he was only fifteen years old at the time, so great was the Grenville charisma. His occupancy of the Isles of Scilly as Governor there successfully pinned down a considerable Parliamentary naval and land force, while his finger was in every move and plan to restore the King. It was through John's cousin, Monck, and Monck's brother Nicholas that John's contacts with the exiled Charles II helped to bring about conditions favourable to the King's return. John had in fact purposely appointed Nicholas Monck as parson of his family living at Kilkhampton in 1653, expressly stipulating that 'he should serve the Publick' with his brother the General if the opportunity arose.

The spacious church at Kilkhampton is full of reminders of the Grenville family. Sir Bevil was brought back from Lansdowne, where there is a monument at the spot at which he was killed, and in 1714 an elaborate memorial was erected to him in the church by his grandson. Sir John, Bevil's son (he was knighted at Bristol in 1643), alas, has no commemoration of this kind at Kilkhampton.

Many grand titles and lucrative appointments were bestowed upon John by a grateful monarch. Shortly after the Restoration he was created Earl of Bath, Viscount Lansdowne, Baron Grenville of Kilkhampton and Bideford, and among lesser roles Governor of Plymouth. This last he took seriously and was closely involved in the building of the Citadel, where his coat of arms may be seen in the great gateway and his name deeply cut into the granite of the foundation stone with the date 1666. It is perhaps something of a memorial to him, and a sign of the triumph of the cause he served so faithfully.

And Anthony Payne? He too shared in the Grenville radiance, being appointed by his master as Halberdier of the Guns at the Citadel of Plymouth, and as Yeoman of the King's Guard by Charles II himself. His portrait was painted by Sir Godfrey Kneller by order of the King, and after many vicissitudes it has come to rest at the Truro Museum, where it may be seen today.

But all this glory and the resounding titles do not do more to compel Cornishmen to revere the memory of these Grenvilles and their associates in the Civil War than does the bright record of their impressive, stirring leadership and unfaltering loyalty in a most splendid moment in the history of the Cornish people.

Bevil's memorial in Kilkhampton Church placed by his grandson in 1714.